❖ WOODHEAD ❖
The Lost Railway

Stephen Gay

The **Hallamshire** Press 1999

©1999 Stephen Gay and The Hallamshire Press

Published by The Hallamshire Press Limited
Broom Hall
Sheffield S10 2DR
England

Typeset by The Hallamshire Press Limited
Printed in Singapore

British Library Cataloguing in Publication Data:

A catalogue record for this book is available from the British Library

ISBN 1 874718 43 1

CONTENTS

In memory of my uncle, Peter Gregory,
who always found my railway photography and travels interesting.

FOREWORD

The Woodhead route between Manchester and Sheffield was an integral part of the coast-to-coast route of the Manchester, Sheffield & Lincolnshire Railway (later the Great Central Railway) by which the large commercial, manufacturing, coal-getting and metal-producing centres on either side of the Pennines were connected. From the 1840s onwards it provided a link for these centres to receive and distribute all manner of goods and materials and, of course, members of the public. This route over the backbone of England was built at considerable human cost and, when modernised approximately 100 years later, was the epitome of traffic operation, assisted at each end by receiving and forwarding points to other areas of the railway network.

However, the decline of the railway was to follow all too quickly. Possibly it was modernised too early, for the equipment was soon deemed non-standard—electrical practice had moved on to more efficient means of distribution and power. Coupled with this was the increasing trend towards direct deliveries offered by road carriers, a trend which originated post World War I but which considerably quickened after World War II. Added to this already formidable change was the global impact of much lower bulk sea rates which made oil a far more attractive fuel, to the detriment of local coal. In addition, the trend for individuals to want more control over their own movements led to the constant rise of car ownership which, in turn, was to lead to the building of the M62 motorway over the Pennines.

Of course, all this happened some years ago now, but with traffic congestion and pollution now high on the political agenda, there has recently been a reappraisal of rail usage. However, considerable damage had already been done to the rail network, with the Woodhead route amongst the many casualties. Would this route be closed in present circumstances one may ask?

In this book, Stephen Gay, who is well known in Pennine circles for his recording of past and present railway routes and their operation, portrays the Woodhead line and its surroundings through the medium of his camera. He illustrates vividly the contrasts to be seen on this route over the Pennines, from the urban environment of one major city, Manchester, over and through the bleak moorland, then down the more sheltered and peaceful valleys before once again returning to an urban landscape, this time that of the city of Sheffield—and all this in a short distance of only thirty or so miles. Many a passenger must have stopped reading his or her newspaper to look out of the carriage window as the train sped down from the summit, for beauty was to be seen whatever the season.

In reading Stephen's book we can share in his obvious passion for this railway—and be reminded of our national follies.

Bryan Longbone
BTech., M.Sc.

ACKNOWLEDGEMENTS

Over the last few years, whilst I was out and about photographing between Manchester and Sheffield, the thought of having this work published never entered my mind. But, through presenting slide shows to various enthusiasts and groups, and receiving very encouraging feedback from them, the possibility of this book came about.

Each of my photographs is complemented with selective information which has been gathered from various sources including retired railwaymen, railway personnel of today, chance meetings with many interesting people and of course from the Great Central Railway Society, for which I am the Northern Area Representative.

I am extremely grateful to the following for their help and assistance in compiling this book:

Denise Herring, Sheffield
Graham Hague, Sheffield
Bryan Longbone, Scunthorpe
Martin Tonge, Hadfield
Peter Hall, Glossop
Owen Russell, Glossop
Derek Sandham, Glossop Heritage Centre
Andrew Macfarlane, Altrincham

John Davies, Crowden
Karl Pashley, Barnsley
Adrian Case, Dronfield
Brian Almond, Barton-upon-Humber

Also, many thanks to the Editor of the *Star* newspaper who, over the last few years has published my Woodhead-related letters and also to Peter Harvey and Martin Dawes, who have also published my jottings in their respective *Star* columns. My sincere thanks also go to *BBC Radio Sheffield* presenters, Rony Robinson and Gerry Kersey, who have invited me, on more than one occasion, to talk railways on their respective programmes. Special thanks also to Liz Oldfield and all the staff at the *South Yorkshire Times* (Mexborough) for the marvellous coverage I get when my railway presentations enter the Dearne Townships! Finally, of course, I must thank Pauline Climpson and the staff of *The Hallamshire Press*.

My biggest thanks though must surely go to Thunder, my seven-year-old German Shepherd. Without his faithful assistance and companionship I would never have ventured around the back streets of Manchester, or tackled the lonely moors over Woodhead—let alone have waited over three hours to photograph a train passing through Beeley Wood!

PREFACE

It was in May, 1971, that I first became interested in railways and, with a school friend, spent many a summer evening 'spotting' at nearby Rotherwood sidings. Rotherwood was the most easterly point for Woodhead electrics and these freight sidings were always full of activity. Electrification reached here in 1955 thus making Rotherwood a motive power changing point between the Woodhead electrics, steam, and latterly, diesel locomotives.

As the years passed, my interest and love for the railways blossomed, with myself and friends soon becoming seasoned travellers. Day returns from Woodhouse to Retford and Doncaster for starters, followed by longer journeys to places like Birmingham, London and even Scotland. Shortly before leaving school in 1976, I obtained my first camera—a small 110 pocket instamatic job, and from that time I've always carried a camera around with me on my travels.

My first taste of work after leaving school was in a chemist's warehouse on the nearby Dore House industrial estate, Handsworth, and this also offered me the sight and sound of Rotherwood activity. However, my employment ambitions were always directed towards the railway and, in May, 1979, I joined British Rail as a Trackman at Beighton Civil Engineers Depot, Sheffield. Beighton depot was constructed between two main railway lines, with one heading towards Grimsby and Cleethorpes and the other to the Midlands and London. Like Rotherwood, Beighton was full of activity and most of my spare time was spent making use of my camera and listening to the reminiscences of

the older drivers and guards. I found these tales fascinating and I only wish I'd thought at the time to record the conversations on tape.

In 1980, with all this former Great Central Railway activity circulating around in my head, I decided to join the Great Central Railway Society to learn more about the company's history. Looking back, I spent 13 wonderful years at Beighton and my work colleagues were, as the song goes, 'Simply The Best'. But, with railway privatisation looming and our sidings threatened with closure, I thought a transfer was in order. So, from April, 1992, I was working and based with the Doncaster civil engineers, but this time working on the main line, and what a difference that was—high speed trains passing me only feet away! Coincidentally, my transfer to Doncaster found me working at former Great Central 'shrines' such as Cleethorpes, Immingham, New Holland, Barnetby, Frodingham and all places in between. Only a few years earlier I'd been discussing these places at Beighton with the older hands!

After nearly three eventful years at Doncaster I was made redundant, on the scrap heap you could say—just like many a locomotive! Since early 1995 I've been searching for railway employment but to no avail. However, what I have achieved in the last few years is to make a photographic record of former Great Central lines and on all my assignments I've been faithfully accompanied by Thunder, my German Shepherd. Together we've travelled and trekked thousands of miles, many were in the comfort of a warm railway carriage, others out walking across a cold and bleak Woodhead terrain.

My photographs have been compiled to produce illustrated slide shows which I present to various groups and societies, Woodhead being my latest venture. Certain pictures in my collection have taken a great deal of time and patience to achieve the effect and atmosphere that I wanted to capture, correct lighting being the main factor. This work on the Woodhead Railway has been no exception, trying to re-create the mood of a closed railway is one thing but photographing across a bleak and desolate moor is another! For interest I have included the date on which each photograph was taken. Hopefully, I have succeeded in capturing the essence of a once-great railway and perhaps the pictures may inspire you, too, to discover *Woodhead-The Lost Railway*.

Stephen Gay

Darnall, Sheffield
April, 1999

ABBREVIATIONS

C.L.C.	Cheshire Lines Committee	L.N.E.R.	London & North Eastern Railway
D.M.U.	Diesel Multiple Unit	L. & N.W.	London & North Western Railway
E.W.S.	English Welsh & Scottish	L. & Y.	Lancashire & Yorkshire Railway
G.C.R.	Great Central Railway	M.S. & L.	Manchester Sheffield & Lincolnshire Railway
G.C. & MID Jt	Great Central & Midland Joint Railway	S.A. & M.	Sheffield Ashton-under-Lyne & Manchester Railway
G.C.R.S.	Great Central Railway Society		

WOODHEAD — THE LOST RAILWAY

The journey begins…

INTRODUCTION

The lifting of tracks does not obliterate a railway—it simply removes its life, leaving a corpse.

Colin Walker, author of *Main Line Lament*, 1973.

For centuries Woodhead has been synonymous with the transportation of goods. Even the Domesday Book gives details on the conveyance of large quantities of salt which were pulled across the lonely moorland by horse and cart—salt being a major commodity and therefore making a lucrative business a thousand years ago. Roads across the Pennines then were very basic, with stone flags laid across marshy areas and guide stoops to prevent horses getting bogged down. In the winter months especially, the journey from South Yorkshire to the Cheshire salt works was very slow, laborious and dangerous, with the 120 mile round trip, taking anything between four and six days to complete.

Hundreds of years later, with the boom of industrialisation, the towns of Manchester and Sheffield were in need of a more direct and efficient transportation link across the Pennines. Various plans, ideas and routes were mooted which included, in November, 1824, a canal linking Sheffield with the Peak Forest Canal at Hyde near Manchester. The route for this canal, via Wortley, Penistone, Woodhead and Mottram, was drawn up by the eminent civil engineer Thomas Telford. Pursuing, initially, the right bank of the River Don from Sheffield northwards, the canal would have crossed the Don no less than seven times between Sheffield and Penistone, eventually reaching the proposed summit under Windleden Cross. A succession of 80 locks would have been needed between Sheffield and the summit, and 66 on the western side, with each lock being approximately 10 feet deep. The proposed length of the canal was $48^{1/2}$ miles, and the rise a total of 1,800ft—between four and five hundred feet higher than the Peak Forest Canal. The proposed 'Sheffield & Manchester Junction Canal' was obviously a far too ambitious and costly affair and, needless to say, the idea of this canal was not pursued. Even if it had been built one wonders how many days it would have been frozen over in winter months.

Ten years later, the Sheffield, Ashton-under-Lyne & Manchester Railway was formed and, during May, 1837, an Act of Parliament was passed to enable the construction of a railway across the backbone of England. On December 23rd, 1845, 'Woodhead' the first Trans-Pennine railway was opened linking Manchester with Sheffield, this included the major engineering feature of the first Woodhead Tunnel. In the following year the railway became part of the Manchester, Sheffield & Lincolnshire Railway but soon, with the increase in traffic, the single-bore tunnel became a major bottleneck. In 1847 plans were drawn up for the construction of a second tunnel, parallel with the first, to ease the congestion and early in 1852 the second Woodhead Tunnel was opened. Sadly, during its construction, 28 lives were lost, most being victims of the great cholera epidemic of 1849.

As the years passed, Woodhead fast became an important trunk route and was soon depicted as a thick black line on all railway maps. In the later years of the nineteenth century the Manchester, Sheffield & Lincolnshire Railway went ahead with plans to build their own railway line to London and, from 1897, in anticipation of this achievement, the company became known as the Great Central Railway. The Woodhead route, now with connections to the capital, became even more important.

The Great Central Railway's 'London Extension' opened in 1899 and, with ever-increasing freight traffic now working over Woodhead, extra lines and marshalling yards were developed and new signalling systems installed. At this time the Great Central Railway's chief locomotive engineer was John George Robinson. In 1913, on a visit to the USA, he saw electrification of a railway at first-hand and thought this form of power was ideally suited to the Woodhead route. However, the installation of such a system would be very expensive and, with war imminent, the idea was shelved.

By January 1923, the London & North Eastern Railway Company had taken over the G.C.R. and a new era had dawned. A few years later, in 1926, the L.N.E.R. looked at the possibility of electrifying the Woodhead line, but the company felt other schemes were more urgent. A start was made on the scheme before war intervened again then, shortly before the end of World War II, work resumed on the electrification. Also included in the scheme were long-needed repairs to the twin-bore Woodhead Tunnel, now 100 years old. Decayed and worn out, the tunnels were beyond repair, so a new double-bore tunnel was the only alternative. In June, 1954, the third Woodhead Tunnel was opened. Now, the thriving cities of Manchester and Sheffield were linked by the most modern railway system in Britain and the first all-electric main line.

In March 1963, the infamous Dr Beeching published his report, *The Reshaping of British Railways*. Two years later, 24 trains per day were diverted from the Woodhead route to run from Sheffield Midland via the Hope Valley line to Manchester. In June, 1967, it was proposed to withdraw all passenger services operating via Woodhead but, following a public outcry, this fast and efficient service was kept running a few years longer, until January 5th, 1970— also the date of the closure of Sheffield Victoria.

Apart from weekend diversions, specials and excursions, the Woodhead route was now a freight artery only, and even that traffic was in fast decline. Various factors were put forward as being responsible for this drastic slump, including the oil crisis, steel strike and alternative routing. My own personal theory for the running down of Woodhead is that it was simply a political sacrifice. From the mid 1970s onwards British Rail had made known their desire to close Woodhead as a through route and, on July 20th, 1981, (which incidentally was the date of my 21st birthday) it was finally closed.

The following pages are my own personal tribute to *Woodhead-The Lost Railway*.

WOODHEAD ROUTE AND CONNECTIONS 1999

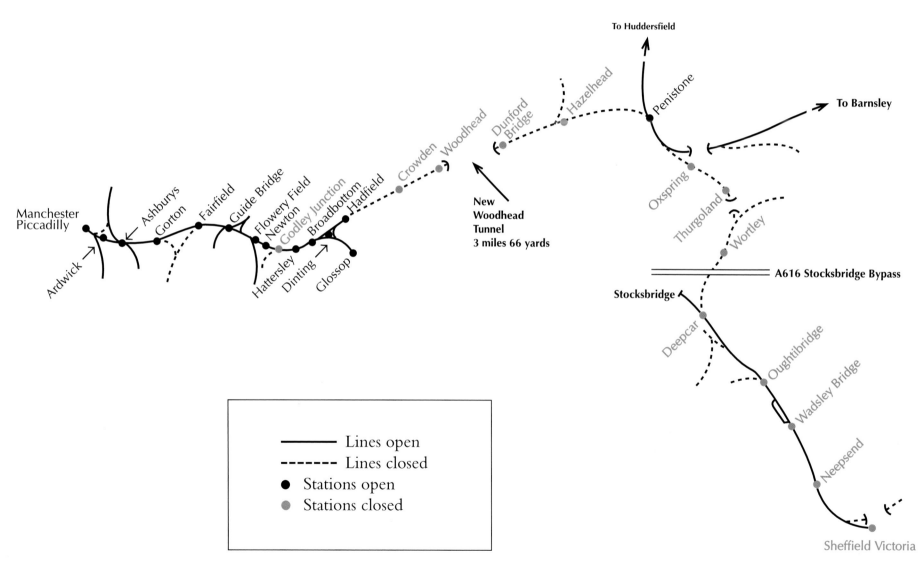

THE WOODHEAD ROUTE — GRADIENT PROFILE

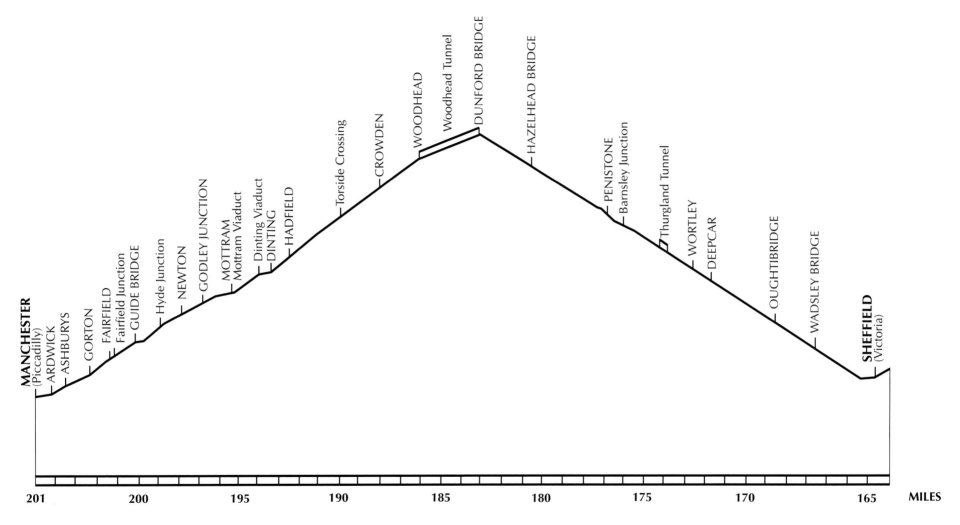

An engineering feature of the day built across a tortuous terrain, construction of Woodhead must surely have taken men to the limit of human endurance.

(Route mileage from London Marylebone Station.)

WOODHEAD ELECTRIFIED LINE MAP 1954

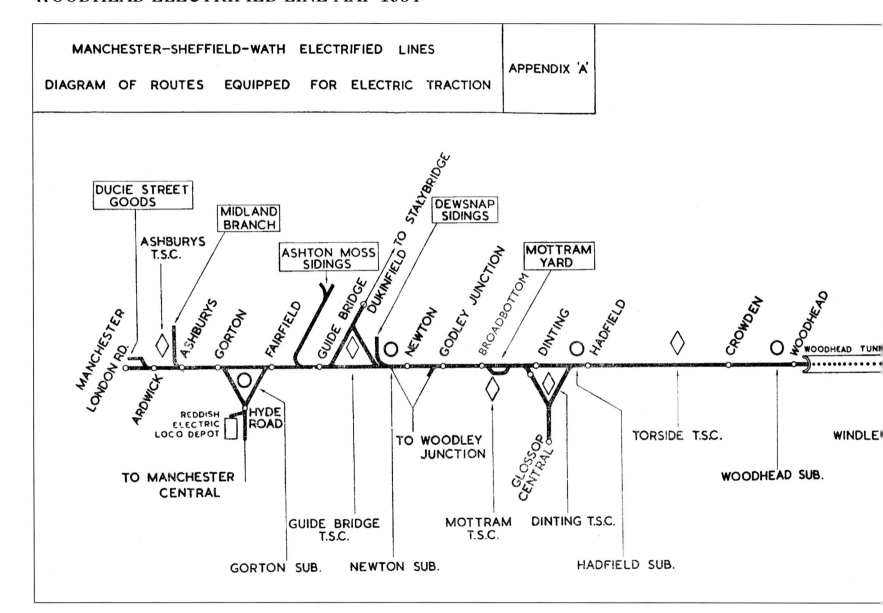

MANCHESTER–SHEFFIELD–WATH ELECTRIFIED LINES	APPENDIX 'A'
DIAGRAM OF ROUTES EQUIPPED FOR ELECTRIC TRACTION	

DUCIE STREET GOODS

MIDLAND BRANCH

DEWSNAP SIDINGS

ASHBURYS T.S.C.

ASHTON MOSS SIDINGS

DUKINFIELD TO STALYBRIDGE

MOTTRAM YARD

MANCHESTER LONDON RD.

ASHBURYS

GORTON

FAIRFIELD

GUIDE BRIDGE

DUKINFIELD

NEWTON

GODLEY JUNCTION

BROADBOTTOM

DINTING

HADFIELD

CROWDEN

WOODHEAD

WOODHEAD TUNNEL

ARDWICK

REDDISH ELECTRIC LOCO DEPOT

HYDE ROAD

TO WOODLEY JUNCTION

GLOSSOP CENTRAL

TORSIDE T.S.C.

WINDLE

TO MANCHESTER CENTRAL

GUIDE BRIDGE T.S.C.

MOTTRAM T.S.C.

DINTING T.S.C.

WOODHEAD SUB.

GORTON SUB.

NEWTON SUB.

HADFIELD SUB.

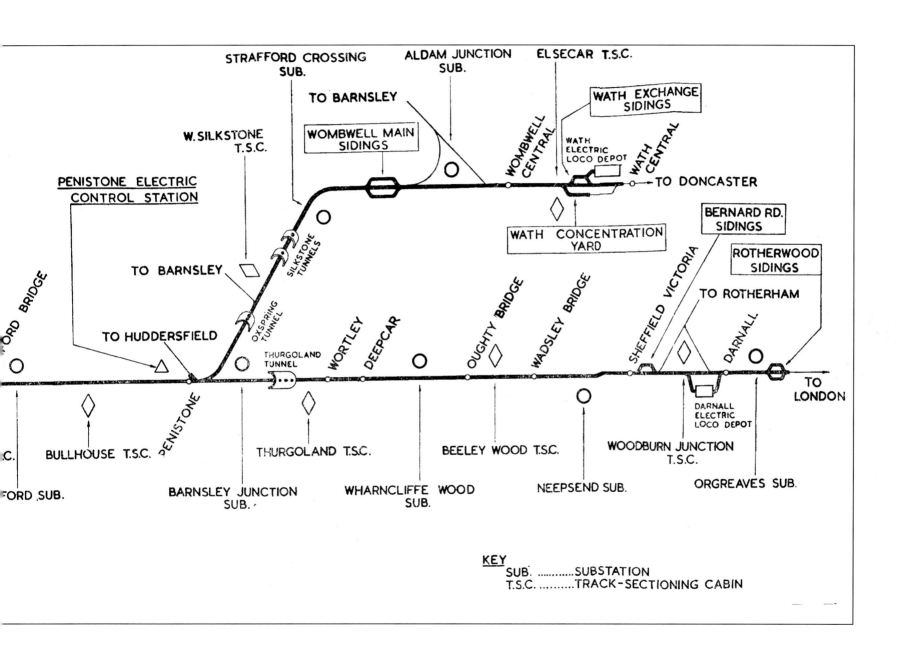

STRAFFORD CROSSING SUB.

ALDAM JUNCTION SUB.

ELSECAR T.S.C.

TO BARNSLEY

WATH EXCHANGE SIDINGS

W. SILKSTONE T.S.C.

WOMBWELL MAIN SIDINGS

WATH ELECTRIC LOCO DEPOT

WOMBWELL CENTRAL

WATH CENTRAL

PENISTONE ELECTRIC CONTROL STATION

SILKSTONE TUNNELS

WATH CONCENTRATION YARD

TO DONCASTER

BERNARD RD. SIDINGS

ROTHERWOOD SIDINGS

TO BARNSLEY

OXSPRING TUNNEL

SHEFFIELD VICTORIA

TO ROTHERHAM

TO HUDDERSFIELD

THURGOLAND TUNNEL

WORTLEY

DEEPCAR

OUGHTY BRIDGE

WADSLEY BRIDGE

DARNALL

FORD BRIDGE

PENISTONE

TO LONDON

DARNALL ELECTRIC LOCO DEPOT

BULLHOUSE T.S.C.

THURGOLAND T.S.C.

BEELEY WOOD T.S.C.

WOODBURN JUNCTION T.S.C.

ORGREAVES SUB.

FORD SUB.

BARNSLEY JUNCTION SUB.

WHARNCLIFFE WOOD SUB.

NEEPSEND SUB.

KEY
SUB. ....SUBSTATION
T.S.C. ....TRACK-SECTIONING CABIN

MANCHESTER PICCADILLY

Thursday, 16th April, 1998

Manchester Piccadilly, the start of the journey, and a look at the 1960's architecture which was all part of a British Railways' modernisation programme for the station. The centrepiece, Rail House, was completed in 1961 but, due to a shortage of funds, it wasn't until 1966 that the rest of the station improvements were completed, so allowing the new look Piccadilly to be officially opened.

From the Manchester, Sheffield & Lincolnshire Railway (M.S. & L. Ry) days, the station was shared with the London & North Western Railway (L. & N.W. Ry) and was called Manchester, London Road, but the station was re-named 'Piccadilly' in September, 1960, in connection with the introduction of 25kV electrification between London Euston and the London Midland Region of British Railways.

Saturday 2nd May, 1998

In through the station's automatic doors to be greeted with the hustle and bustle of a modern station. Today's station concourse is more like a shopping centre with its array of boutiques and burger bars. To me this station seems far too congested.

Thursday, 16th April, 1998

Manchester Piccadilly's spectacular roof, which is supported by ornate columns, is presently being refurbished at a cost of £33 million. The project will use 220 miles of scaffolding tube and a total of 13,000 panes of glass. The roof works are scheduled for completion in the summer of 1999, with the whole scheme set to finish in time for the Millennium.

Seen departing from No. 2 platform, is the late-running 0816 Manchester Piccadilly–Marple service.

Thursday, 16th April, 1998

Other recent improvements at Manchester Piccadilly have included new platform lighting, track and signalling work. The aim is to increase capacity and prevent congestion at the station.

Seen departing, again from No. 2 platform, later the same day is Heritage Class 10, one unit, working the 1824 service to Rose Hill Marple. To the right of the picture, and almost hidden by modern city architecture, is the surviving Great Central Railway Goods Depot in Ducie Street.

DUCIE STREET
GOODS DEPOT

Thursday 16th April, 1998

The Goods Depot was opened by the M.S. & L. Ry in the 1870s and closed in October 1967. Today this fine building is listed and stands alongside the entrance to an NCP car park.

The L. & N.W. Ry also boasted a Goods Depot fronting onto Ducie Street, this closed in May 1965. Sadly, by 1966, it had been demolished to make way for the seven-storey office block, Gateway House, which opened in 1968.

ARDWICK JUNCTION

Wednesday, 16th April, 1998

Departing from Piccadilly over the many points and crossings it is a mere $^1/_2$ mile to the first point of interest, Ardwick Junction. The former L. & N.W. line to Stockport and beyond continues south along the main line leaving the Woodhead route to head in an easterly direction.

Pictured here rounding onto the Woodhead route proper, is the 0725 Manchester Piccadilly–Hull service, these Liverpool/Manchester–North East workings began running via Ardwick and Guide Bridge from May 15th, 1989. Also of note on the right are the overgrown railway arches which once carried the former Lancashire & Yorkshire Railway from Miles Platting. This line closed between Ardwick Junction and Ashburys Midland Junction in September, 1964.

ARDWICK

Thursday, 29th May, 1997

Ardwick is a little used station only a stone's throw from Piccadilly. It was originally of the staggered platform design, but today is a simple island affair.

On Table 84 in the current Great Britain Passenger Timetable (Manchester–Glossop & Hadfield) only two services per weekday call at Ardwick. On the following table, 85, (Sheffield, New Mills & Marple to Manchester) things are a little healthier with eight services calling, but again only on weekdays!

Seen here passing through, is the 1308 Manchester Piccadilly–Marple service, one of the many trains which do not call at this seemingly forgotten station.

Wednesday, 9th July, 1997

Three-car Class 158 passing through with the 0623 Manchester Airport–York service.

Note the island platform, one of only two between Manchester and Hadfield. Also of note is the unusual platform surface!

ASHBURYS WEST JUNCTION

Wednesday, 9th July, 1997

Departing from Ardwick, a Class 101 Heritage Unit passes the once-extensive Great Central Railway sidings on the approach to Ashburys West Junction, while working the 0720 Manchester Piccadilly–Marple service.

Thursday, 16th April, 1998

On the approach to Ashburys station, a two-car Class 101 Heritage Unit passes Ashburys West Junction with the 0700 Manchester Piccadilly–Sheffield service. This is the point where the Midland Railway branched off to serve its goods depots at Ashton Road and Ancoats, before joining up with the L. & Y. on the Miles Platting branch.

Trains to
New Mills Central,
Rose Hill, Marple,
Glossop, Hadfield ↗

Thursday, 16th April, 1998

Formerly called 'Ashburys for Belle Vue' this station is today void of any architectural features of yesteryear. The original buildings, which dated from the 1850s, were all demolished in 1994 to help make way for the nearby inner ring road.

Thankfully many commuter trains still call at this now unstaffed station including, on this occasion, the 1730 Manchester Piccadilly–New Mills Central service.

Thursday 16th April, 1998

Ashburys East Junction is the point where services to
Romiley and New Mills Central branch right along the
former Great Central & Midland Railway Joint. In 1984
Ashburys West signal box closed and from that same
date (6.5.84) a new panel was commissioned in
Ashburys East box, which today is simply called
Ashburys.

Seen here shortly after departure from Ashburys, and
about to branch right, is the 1738 Manchester
Piccadilly–Rose Hill Marple service.

GORTON

Wednesday, 23rd October, 1996

From Ashburys it is a short distance, only one mile, to Gorton, passing on the left the former G.C.R. Locomotive Carriage and Waggon Works which today is home to the new Manchester Wholesale Fruit & Vegetable Market.

Directly opposite this famous works was another world-renowned railway foundry, that of Messrs Beyer, Peacock & Company. Today, they too are just a memory. This picture was obtained (with kind permission of the caretaker) by standing on the roof of Cornwall House, a block of flats 240ft high!

Wednesday, 23rd October, 1996

Moving the camera a little right, the next picture of Gorton is dominated by Verna Street School, also in the picture is the dried-up remains (Stockport branch) of the Manchester & Ashton-under-Lyne Canal. Originally this aqueduct crossed the railway on stone arches but, with the widening of the main line between Ardwick and Hyde Junction in 1906, a replacement aqueduct was installed. Sadly this section of canal became derelict in the 1950s.

Wednesday, 23rd October, 1996

Gorton station, formerly called 'Gorton and Openshaw'—again viewed from Cornwall Court. Looking down to see a three-car Class 305 (slam door stock) seen awaiting departure for Glossop and Hadfield.

So much for the Great Central's planned 1902 widening between Manchester and Hyde Junction. Today it is back to just two tracks. On the right hand side, just after Lees Street overbridge, is the former Gorton Junction where the Great Central branched towards Hyde Road Junction, through Fallowfield and on towards the Cheshire Lines at Chorlton.

GORTON JUNCTION

Saturday, 14th February, 1998

Today Gorton Junction is no more, having closed completely through to Trafford Park Junction in October 1988 and, after three years of rusting, line track lifting commenced in September 1991.

A sorry sight indeed, as we see a three-car Class 323 accelerating away with the 1003 Manchester Piccadilly–Hadfield/Glossop service.

FAIRFIELD

Monday, 9th March, 1998

The station 'Fairfield for Droylsden' opened in 1892 and is said to have boasted more platforms than London Marylebone! Fairfield Junction completed the 'Gorton Triangle' but this section, to Hyde Road Junction, closed over five years earlier in May, 1983.

The 1018 Manchester Piccadilly–Rose Hill Marple service departs, passing the site of the former Fairfield Junction.

GUIDE BRIDGE

Arrival at Guide Bridge, five miles after leaving Manchester, a place which, years ago, could be called the Clapham Junction of the North West. Between 1845 and 1905 many lines were constructed, some passing through, some crossing over and even one line passing below, thus developing Guide Bridge into a very important rail centre.

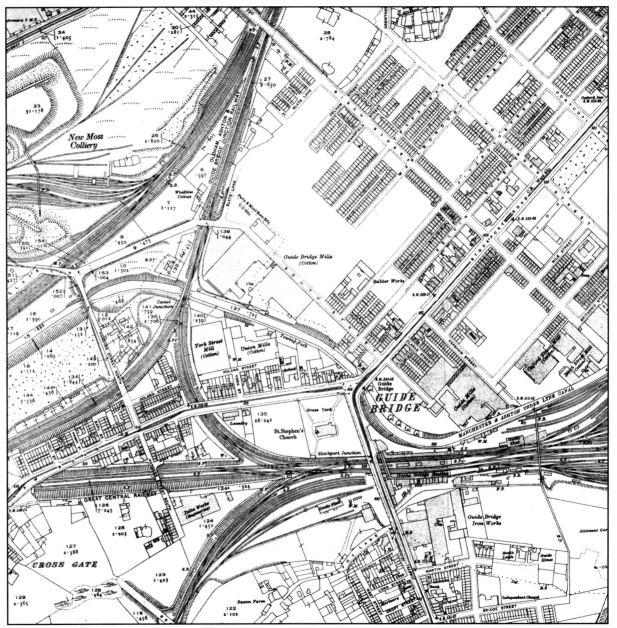

Extract from Lancashire Sheet 105.10, 1918, courtesy of Alan Godfrey Maps.

Saturday, 2nd May 1998

Sadly, today, much of that importance has faded away, but many traces of the past can still be discovered. Continuing on from Fairfield, the first points of interest are these two surviving bridge abutments that once carried the L. & N.W. Ry between Ashton Moss Junction and Droylsden (L. & Y.). The overbridge in the background carries the line between Denton Junction and Ashton Moss Junction, which is still in use today.

Another line used to run here, the Oldham, Ashton & Guide Bridge Junction Ry (which was a joint affair with the L. & N.W. and the M.S. & L.). This line branched off at Audenshaw Junction, which was located just after the L. & N.W. overbridge on the left and ran via Oldham Road, Park Bridge, to Oldham, Clegg Street Station.

Wednesday, 9th July, 1997

With St Stephen's church dominating the skyline, just like it has graced so many railway photographs over the years, two Class 101 Heritage units pause together at Guide Bridge.

On the left, the 1112 Rose Hill Marple–Manchester Piccadilly service and on the right, the 1120 Manchester Piccadilly–Rose Hill Marple service.

Monday, 15th July, 1996

Prior to the electric conversion from 1500V DC to 25kV AC, the Guide Bridge area was resignalled in December 1984 and the fast lines through the station were taken out of use. Today, all the Guide Bridge area is controlled by one signal box, which is the former Ashton Junction box, now simply called Guide Bridge.

Friday, 30th May, 1997

Demolition and enlargement of Guide Bridge Station around 1905 paved the way for more spacious and improved facilities. Sadly, the hustle and bustle of the thousands of passengers who used these grand buildings is no more. Boarded-up and silent, but thankfully just about graffiti-free, the buildings await an uncertain future.

Tuesday, 19th August, 1997

A Class 60, seen crossing the original stone viaduct built in 1841, on the approach to Guide Bridge East Junction with empties for Peak Forest Sorting Sidings near Buxton. 64 years after the building of the bridge, in January, 1905, the Great Central Railway decided to lay another connection in the area, this ran from Guide Bridge East to Guide Bridge North Jc.

Another line would once have featured in this picture, the L. & N.W. Stalybridge Junction Line, which branched just north of Denton Jc., ran through a short tunnel under the G.C. then continued alongside the River Tame to Dukinfield and on to Stalybridge.

January, 1998

Shortly after passing Guide Bridge East Junction the Peak Forest Canal is crossed. This canal was opened in 1800 linking the Ashton Canal, at Dukinfield Bridge, with the Peak Forest Tramway at Buxworth.

This 14½ mile waterway was constructed during 'Canal Mania' when canals were being built all over the country and, like so many others, it was taken over in later years by a railway company. Incidentally, the Peak Forest Canal is one of the oldest components of the Great Central Railway. It was incorporated on March 28th, 1794, and acquired by the Sheffield, Ashton-under-Lyne & Manchester Railway, on March 25th, 1846.

FLOWERY FIELD

Wednesday, 10th February, 1999

Hadfield-bound Class 323 entering Flowery Field Station, with the 1353 service from Manchester Piccadilly.

Flowery Field is a relatively new station on the Railtrack system, it was opened on May 13th, 1985. This two-platform affair was supposedly only an experiment, but fourteen years on it's still open and serving well the communities of Newton and Hyde.

North West Trains introduced the Class 323s on Manchester Piccadilly–Glossop/Hadfield services in November, 1997, and to accommodate these three-car units, platform extensions had to be made at Flowery Field and other stations en route.

HYDE JUNCTION

Friday, 15th August, 1997

Three-car Class 305, passing Hyde Junction, with the 1825 Manchester Piccadilly–Hadfield service.

Hyde Junction, is the point where the G.C. & MID Jt. line branches towards Hyde Central, Woodley and Romiley.

This view is from the very end of Hyde North station platform.

NEWTON STATION

Wednesday, 10th September, 1997

Newton Station is the next stop and with only a matter of weeks left on Manchester–Glossop/Hadfield line services, a Class 305 arrives with the 1625 from Manchester Piccadilly.

Wednesday, 10th September, 1997

Formerly called 'Newton for Hyde' the station nameboards of today read simply 'Newton' although in the current Great Britain Passenger Timetable, on table No. 84, it is still listed 'Newton for Hyde'!

This station is 7½ miles from Manchester and this was the first section of the Woodhead line, which opened in 1841. In those early days station buildings and facilities would have been limited but, in 1883, the M.S. & L. Ry improved the station giving us the grand and elegant architecture which survives to this day complete with the company's initials and date stone which grace these fine Victorian buildings.

Also surviving at Newton is the equally impressive high retaining wall and the adjacent coal drops which once supported the very busy goods yard. Three-car Class 305, departs from its Newton stop with the 1525 Manchester Piccadilly–Hadfield service.

Departing from Newton the line crosses the viaduct then shortly afterwards crosses what has been called Britain's biggest white elephant, the M67 motorway, dubbed the 'Road to Nowhere'!

GODLEY

Monday, 13th April, 1998

Just a short one-mile sprint away is Godley Station. Like Flowery Field Station, Godley is relatively new, it replaced the old East Station. Today, it is rare to see a D.M.U. east of Hyde Junction, so I was pleased to capture this set working the 1443, Manchester Piccadilly–Hadfield service.

GODLEY JUNCTION

Saturday, 1st November, 1997

Godley Junction Station, which opened on February 1st, 1866, was a place once surrounded by marshalling yards full of activity, it was the exchange point between steam, diesel and electric traction. As well as freight, the station had a full complement of passenger services. Sadly, as illustrated by this picture, that is not the case today.

Re-named simply 'Godley' on May 6th, 1974, the station had yet another name change on May 11th, 1987, when it became known as 'Godley East'. The reason being that on that date, as previously mentioned, the present Godley Station opened. From May the following year the passenger service at Godley East was non-existent, apart from one solitary service per week—the then infamous (SO) 1238 Hadfield–Manchester Piccadilly! The reason for keeping on just one passenger train was due to an Act of Parliament which prevented B.R. (as it was then) from closing a station or abandoning a service, without consent of the Secretary of State for Transport. Inevitably, time caught up with Godley East and the station officially closed on Saturday, May 27th, 1995.

This is also the appropriate point to mention that Godley Junction was the most easterly point of the 'Cheshire Lines Committee', a railway comprising of the Great Central; Great Northern; & Midland companies. Looking at this picture, the C.L.C. platforms towards Woodley and Stockport would have been to the left, but sadly, today, they are just a fond memory.

HATTERSLEY

Wednesday, 10th September, 1997

Having just passed through the island platform affair
of Hattersley Station, which was opened by Greater
Manchester P.T.E. on May 8th, 1978, the 1425
Manchester Piccadilly–Hadfield service enters a deep
cutting. Prior to 1928, to take this picture, I would have
been standing above Hattersley No. 2 tunnel
(approximately 150yds) looking down towards the
shorter Hattersley No. 1 tunnel (55yds). Between 1928
and 1931 these two crumbling tunnels were opened
out as the wall linings were decaying due to excessive
amounts of water seepage.

MOTTRAM VIADUCT

BROADBOTTOM

Wednesday, 28th May, 1997

Having just arrived at the delightful and restored Broadbottom Station, Class 305 awaits departure with the 0955 Manchester Piccadilly–Hadfield service. The ticket office is still staffed, albeit on a part-time basis, and the former Station Master's accommodation is now home to the Broadbottom Station pub restaurant where,

in their Pullman Lounge, they serve scrumptious meals and have a fine selection of real ales.

In November, 1997, on behalf of the Great Central Railway Society, I presented an illustrated slide show in these delightful buildings. It's an evening I shall remember for a very long time, friendly staff, an excellent meal, real ale and a good crowd!

Saturday, 7th July, 1984

Back to 1984 for this picture, which features a fondly remembered L.N.E.R. designed Class 506 unit, crossing Mottram Viaduct. The service is the 1943 Hadfield–Manchester Piccadilly, obviously in the opposite direction of our journey, but nevertheless it illustrates the very impressive structure which crosses the River Ethrow 120ft below and crosses the border into Derbyshire.

MOTTRAM STAFF HALT

Wednesday, 4th February, 1998

In 1930, the L.N.E.R. announced plans to construct a new marshalling yard at Mottram to replace the existing sidings at Guide Bridge and Godley, they had become unsuitable for the large amounts of traffic the L.N.E.R. were handling at that time.

Opened in 1935, this vast complex also boasted its own station—a Trainmen's Halt, its proper term. Sadly today, that is about all that survives. Interestingly, Mottram Staff Halt is still shown as 'Open' in current Working Timetables and the latest edition of the O.P.C. Rail Atlas!

MOTTRAM

Thursday, 29th May, 1997

Running over the, now-closed, Mottram Yard is the Glossop Road overbridge—or 'Gamesley Bridge' to the natives. The bridge makes a fine vantage point for railway photography. Here, pointing the camera east, a Class 305 heading towards Dinting with the 1825 Manchester Piccadilly–Hadfield service can be seen about to cross another impressive viaduct.

Mention must be made here of the 'Waterside Branch' built in 1879 by the M.S. & L. Ry. This steeply graded two-mile line was built to serve the textile mills near Hadfield and Tintwistle, the branch closed completely on July 20th, 1965.

DINTING VIADUCT

Wednesday, 9th July, 1997

Mention 'Woodhead' to most railway enthusiasts and the famous tunnels would undoubtedly spring to mind but not far behind in their thoughts would be this structure—the famous Dinting Vale Viaduct. Victorian civil engineering at its very best, 119ft high and 1,200ft wide.

Opened in August 1844, it consisted of four stone piers, approaching arches either side and was of timber construction. In 1860, the timber was replaced with wrought iron box girders and then, years later, just as at Mottram Viaduct, seven brick-strengthening piers were added between 1918 and 1920.

Today, even with the added piers, the structure still looks impressive as a Class 305 rumbles over with the 1755 Manchester Piccadilly–Hadfield service.

Saturday, 7th July, 1984

Back to 1984 for another view of this masterpiece (taken from the opposite side) with a Class 506 crossing while working the 2043 Hadfield–Manchester Piccadilly service.

Exactly five months after this picture was taken, all Class 506 units were withdrawn from service due to the line's conversion from 1500V DC to 25kV AC.

DINTING WEST JUNCTION

Friday, 30th May, 1997

Branching off the main line at Dinting West Junction straight after crossing the viaduct, for the short journey to Glossop, the 1925 Manchester Piccadilly–Hadfield service enters Dinting Station.

DINTING STATION

Friday, 30th May, 1997

Dinting Station's history involves a complexity of names, dates, owners and parliamentary acts but, in brief, a station first opened at Dinting in December, 1842. The present station buildings date from 1884, with the west–south curve being installed by the M.S. & L. Ry that same year. Awaiting departure on this very sharp curve is the 1855 Manchester Piccadilly–Hadfield service.

DINTING LANE CROSSING

Saturday, 25th April, 1998

Approaching Dinting Lane Crossing is the 1637 Manchester Piccadilly–Hadfield service.

This one-mile branch line was originally single and a private line for the Duke of Norfolk. A year after its construction, in 1846, the branch was taken over by the Sheffield, Ashton-under-Lyne and Manchester Railway. The line was doubled in 1883, with a single road engine shed being provided at Dinting. The 1637 Manchester Piccadilly–Hadfield service approaches the now fixed level-crossing gates.

DINTING ENGINE SHED

Saturday, 25th April, 1998

Thirty years ago the old M.S. & L. Ry single road engine shed, once a sub-shed of Gorton, was home of the Dinting Railway Centre a place operated by The Bahamas Locomotive Society. Sadly, after years of arguments over land, money and all the usual preservation pitfalls the Centre is no more.

GLOSSOP STATION

Thursday, 29th May, 1997

The 2008 Hadfield–Manchester Piccadilly service awaits departure from Glossop.

Glossop's 'Central' suffix was dropped from May, 1974, but the sign outside the station survives to this day!

LOWER DINTING

Thursday, 16th April, 1998

Approaching Lower Dinting a Class 323 unit makes easy work of the climb from Glossop while working the 1303 Manchester Piccadilly–Hadfield service. With rationalisation of trackwork in 1969, the railway between Glossop Central and Dinting became single line working.

DINTING SOUTH JUNCTION

Monday, 13th April, 1998

Passing Dinting South Junction, a Class 323 working the 15.23 Manchester Piccadilly–Hadfield service. It will avoid Dinting Station by curving sharp right, rejoining the former main line at Dinting East Junction.

DINTING EAST JUNCTION

Wednesday 4th March, 1998

Passing beneath Dinting Road overbridge, the 1558 Manchester Piccadilly–Hadfield service is about to rejoin the former main line.

DINTING STATION

Friday, 30th May, 1997

One more look at Dinting Station, this time a view of the splendid down-line main platform buildings, which again date from 1884.

At the time of writing, Dinting Station signal box is the last to be mechanically operated on the whole Woodhead route between Manchester and Sheffield.

HADFIELD

Wednesday 4th March, 1998

With the Longdendale terrain now in sight, the 1525 Hadfield–Manchester Piccadilly service rushes past away from the threatening thunderous weather.

Thursday, 16th April, 1998

Photographed from Hadfield's Castle Hill, and under another angry sky, the 0943 service from Manchester Piccadilly slows nearing journey's end.

Friday, 30th May 1997

The first part of this journey terminates at Hadfield Station, a distance of 15 miles from Manchester. The station, formerly called 'Hadfield for Hollingworth', is 153 years old and the original Sheffield, Ashton-under-Lyne & Manchester Railway stone buildings are still standing proud.

Saturday, 10th July 1998

Continuing on from Hadfield Station it is time to leave the iron road behind. The next part of the journey is made on foot along the Longdendale Trail, part of the proposed coast-to-coast long distance footpath from Southport to Hull, known as the Trans-Pennine Trail.

VALEHOUSE

Wednesday, 10th February, 1999

The Longdendale Trail between Hadfield and Woodhead was officially opened on May 22nd, 1992, it follows the former Woodhead Railway route which, today, is owned by North West Water and funded by various bodies.

In this picture of Valehouse is Bottoms Reservoir, the first of five reservoirs constructed alongside the railway between 1850 and 1877, providing Manchester with Europe's first major water supply. Actually, the Woodhead, Torside, and Rhodeswood reservoirs provide the drinking water, with Valehouse, and Bottoms providing compensation water for the River Ethrow.

Sunday, 12th April, 1998

From the same Valehouse overbridge but this time looking east, this is the first view of Woodhead's rugged landscape and breath-taking scenery including, on the right, Bramah Edge.

The Woodhead route at this point was constructed alongside the River Ethrow, thus avoiding any unnecessary engineering. The very top of Bramah Edge is over 700ft high and so it is a hard trek to the summit to capture the panoramic view of this beautiful area.

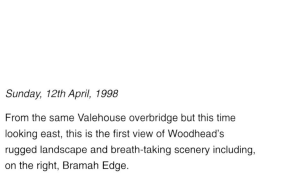

BRAMAH EDGE

Sunday, 12th April, 1998

Looking across to picturesque Tintwistle over Valehouse and Bottoms Reservoirs. Sadly, Tintwistle has become very noisy and dangerous, spoilt by the sheer volume of traffic which thunders through along the A628 Woodhead Pass.

Across the valley, on Woodhead Road, adjacent to Valehouse Wood a tragic inscription can be seen on a stone wall:

BURNED DOWN
TWO CHILDREN
BURNT to DEATH
AGED 3 AND 5 YEARS
AUGUST 17th 1853

These poor souls died after being trapped as a raging fire swept through their small shanty-town house—a large community of navvies lived in this bleak area during the construction of the reservoirs. The cause of the fire had been gross neglect, the jury later returned a verdict of 'accidental death'.

Monday, 11th December, 1995

The weather in the Longdendale Valley can be very changeable, one minute bright and sunny, the next rain, mist and snow. Thunder and I found this out when we were unable to descend from Bramah Edge due to the thick mist which suddenly came down making walking conditions very hazardous. A flask of tea and digestive biscuits, and a photo-call, were the order of the day until conditions improved!

Sunday, 12th April, 1998

When the weather does pick up, the vista is certainly rewarding with a clear view of Torside. Just to the left of this picture another long distance footpath, the Pennine Way, crosses between Torside and Rhodeswood Reservoirs.

CROWDEN

Sunday, 9th June 5 1996

Leaving the Dark Peak mysteries behind, we arrive back on the former trackbed at Crowden, a bleak and lonely place just over 17 miles from Manchester. Apart from a flight of steps which once led down to the footbridge, nothing remains of Crowden Station which was closed by British Railways on February 4th, 1957. However, the four small railway cottages do survive. Well over 100 years old, these small dwellings once provided housing for the station's Ganger, two Signalmen, the Sub-Ganger and their families. Today, only the former Ganger's house, No. 4 Railway Cottages, is occupied, the other three were vacated way back in 1963.

TORSIDE CROSSING

Monday, 13th April, 1998

On January 5th, 1970, regular passenger services between Manchester and Sheffield via Woodhead ceased to operate and the sight of a Sheffield bound service passing Torside crossing became a thing of the past.

Not exactly true, as, on summer Sundays and Bank Holidays, it is still possible to pass over Torside crossing on a Sheffield bound passenger service—albeit only on a bus! Sheffield bus company, Mainline, do the honours, with Peak Park service No. 402 from Glossop.

Before leaving Torside crossing, I'd like to recall an incident which occurred in the area, on Wednesday December 5th, 1956.

The signal box at Torside was located on the up-side and on duty this particular day was relief signalman, Leslie Simpson. At exactly 12.30 p.m., to Mr Simpson's despair, he heard and watched from the warmth of his box, an L-20 type Beaver Communication Plane crash and burst into flames high on the desolate Bramah Edge. Two American airmen were killed.

After the tragic crash Mr Simpson put through an emergency call and a Police team from Glossop rushed to the scene, followed by a rescue party who struggled up the almost vertical hillside. Meanwhile, down below, trains continued to and fro, with passengers unaware of the hilltop tragedy.

Many sightings and reports of low-flying silent ghost planes are common in the area!

NO. 4, RAILWAY COTTAGES

Monday 4th May, 1998

90 years young Mr John Davies is the sole survivor at Railway Cottages and, after living at No. 4 for the last 70 years, John told me he's no intention of moving out!

Born into a railway family, he started work on the L.N.E.R. in 1924 as a messenger lad at Dunford Bridge—or Junior Porter to give him his proper title. After various postings and jobs on the L.N.E.R., British Railways–Eastern Region, and latterly London Midland Region, he retired in December, 1973, as Signalman at Crowden Station.

ST JAMES' CHURCH

Sunday, 9th June 3 1996

Before continuing with the journey a quick look at St James' Church, which nestles on the opposite hillside from Crowden Station, near to where the road from Glossop joins the main A628.

Although in Crowden, for many years the church has been known as Woodhead and dates back to 1487. Many of the navvies killed in the construction of the first Woodhead Tunnels are known to be buried here.

Sunday 8th June, 1986

My visits to the Woodhead area in the 1970s and '80s were few and far between, but one visit to Crowden, in 1986, provided these two pictures which show the permanent way with only weeks to survive.

The first shows a Class 47 heading towards Woodhead to pick up a long-welded-rail train with the next picture showing the convoy heading back towards Manchester.

WOODHEAD

Sunday, 8th June, 1986

June 1986, and a photograph of Woodhead Tunnel before the long-welded-rail train arrives. It is hard to believe that a major engineering feature like this, lasted a mere 27 years in service.

Construction began in February 1949, with work being done by the contracting engineers, Balfour Beatty. Over 1,000 men were employed in the task, with 500,000 cubic yards of rock being excavated. The resulting tunnel walls had a minimum thickness of 21 inches!

The tunnel is driven through poor shale for approximately 80% of its length and through blocky sandstone for the remaining 20%. Because the line was electrically operated, the only ventilation provided was the retention of a 16ft construction shaft (depth 467ft).

Saturday 4th November, 1995

Above its mouth a suitable date stone records the year of achievement. Originally it was planned for our present Queen to officially open the tunnel, but I suppose with all her other commitments the ceremonial honour was left to the then Minister of Transport, Alan Lennox-Boyd.

A plaque commemorating the opening of Woodhead New Tunnel, on June 3rd, 1954, is displayed on Platform 1 at Manchester Piccadilly. Today the tunnel is the property of the National Grid.

Saturday 4th November, 1995

Adjacent to the new Woodhead Tunnel is the original bore (3 miles 22 yards) which was opened in December, 1845, at a cost of £200,000; 157 tons of gunpowder were used to blast a way through the millstone grit, shale and sandstone. The first Woodhead Tunnel soon proved to be a bottleneck and, in 1847, work started on a new bore to accommodate the up-line.

Sadly, the construction was marred by tragedy, and in 1849 a cholera epidemic claimed the lives of 28 navvies. Most, if not all, are buried at St James' Church, Woodhead. On a much brighter note, the second tunnel was opened for traffic on February 2nd, 1852.

As previously mentioned, after over 100 years in use both tunnels became disused, then, in 1963, the C.E.G.B. decided to make use of the old bore, the up tunnel, to carry a 400,000 volt power line. The work included the laying of a 2ft narrow-gauge railway for construction and maintenance purposes.

Sunday, 12th April, 1998

From a position high above the entrances of the Woodhead Tunnels, this view looks back down the beautiful Longdendale Valley.

To accompany the opening of the new electrified tunnel, a new station was opened at Woodhead, but this new station only lasted a little over 10 years, closing completely on July 27th, 1964. It is interesting to note that when closure notices were received, five months earlier, two local councillors visited the station to see how many people used it. Their findings? Only three people used the station on a regular basis and two of them were railway employees! So, with only one fare paying passenger, a male nurse, closure was inevitable. One final point raised at a Chapel-en-le-Frith council meeting, was 'Woodhead Station is not a station, but a Halt for railway servants to do their shopping'!

Monday 4th May, 1998

In addition to the 28 navvies who died from cholera, many were killed by accidents. The first tunnel claimed 26 lives in all, with most coming to grief in gunpowder accidents. Located at Woodhead, and built into the hillside, is the stone cavern that was used to store the tons of gunpowder needed to blast the tunnel through. An eerie place indeed—but well worth a look inside.

Saturday 4th November, 1995

Obviously, access is denied through any of the three tunnels, so, armed with a good walking stick, its up, over the top and across this bleak and desolate moor. For the first tunnel, five ventilation shafts were constructed, varying in depth (between 189 and 135 yards) but all with an 8ft diameter. Approximately half of the excavation was drawn up through these shafts (272,685 cubic yards). The second tunnel made use of this same ventilation, with 25 side arches, or manholes, linking the two.

Four of the five ventilation shafts are still visible, and it is common to see vapour rising from them. This is due to a mixture of condensation, and coolant used on machinery down below.

Saturday, 4th November, 1995

Whenever I stand in the quiet of this desolate moor, I try to imagine the time when over 1,100 men, women and children lived up here in their shanty homes, in the most dreadful of conditions, during the construction of the tunnel.

The impact of such a large body of people must have been enormous on the local area and surrounding villages, yet very little is recorded about their presence—apart from a few inscriptions on the gravestones of those who died!

Also to be seen whilst crossing the moor are these concrete posts. They were used to support theodolites during surveying work for the third tunnel.

SALTER'S BROOK

Saturday, 4th November, 1995

Salter's Brook is just a short detour from the line of the tunnel, and here is the border crossing, on the A628, between South Yorkshire and Derbyshire. The ruins of the former Lady Cross Shooting Lodge are clearly visible, a place used by the gentry of the day during the season. Nearby, but out of picture (right), was the old Millers Arms which closed in 1917. The inn must have been a welcome sight and resting place for the weary traveller.

Sat in amongst the ruins is quite an idyllic setting, a perfect resting place to enjoy a flask of tea and digestive biscuits— that is, of course, if you can find your way in!

Back on line with the tunnel again, at the final ventilation shaft before the descent to Dunford Bridge.

As you can see, some budding Philip Hawkins has been hard at work, painting Class 76 Bo-Bo No. 76001.

Coincidentally, only once have I travelled through Woodhead Tunnel, on Saturday April 8th, 1978, on the 'Great Central Wanderer' from London Marylebone, via High Wycombe, Coventry, and Nuneaton. We travelled to Dinting via many rare freight lines, including a run from Godley Junction to Penistone, and behind which locomotive?—76001!

DUNFORD BRIDGE

Sunday 6th December, 1998

An aerial view of Dunford Bridge from high above the South Yorkshire side of Woodhead Tunnel, the Windle Edge road can be seen climbing away to join the A628 at Salter's Brook. Also in the picture is the famous Stanhope Arms public house, awaiting the first customers of the day!

Between 1949 and 1954, during construction of the third Woodhead Tunnel, several hundred staff were employed, most being housed in a camp of huts. Several amenities were provided, including recreation huts, a cinema, post office, medical and ambulance facilities and more—a busy and active community indeed!

Sunday, 6th December, 1998

Earlier, I mentioned that Woodhead Station had only lasted ten years. Over three miles on, the second Dunford Bridge Station lasted a little longer, closing to passengers on January 5th, 1970, with the loss of services between Manchester and Sheffield.

Nearly thirty years after closure the station is just about recognisable and, sadly, the modern electric railway system is just a memory.

Sunday, 6th December, 1998

The Upper Don Trail, running from Dunford Bridge through Penistone to Oxspring, is a section of the Trans-Pennine Trail. This section of the proposed 205-mile long-distance footpath opened in October, 1998.

Beyond Oxspring, the trail continues east to Silkstone Common, onto the Dove Valley section to Worsbrough, Wombwell, and the Old Moor Wetlands Centre.

In recognition of Dunford Bridge's connection with the railway, a disused 2ft narrow-gauge wagon has been displayed on a section of old siding.

TOWNHEAD

Sunday, 6th December, 1998

A hundred years ago, the Great Central Railway approved the laying of sorting sidings at Dunford Bridge and, after many disputes and wranglings with local landowners, the sidings were opened in this bleak location in March, 1902. To accommodate the increased workforce, a railway community called Townhead was developed.

100 years on, and long after the railway has departed, Townhead survives, complete with the old steps made from railway sleepers which once led many employees from the busy yard, up to two rows of railwaymen's cottages. Today all are home for a contingent of friendly New Age Travellers.

HAZLEHEAD

Sunday, 9th June, 1996

Like Crowden, Hazlehead must have been a very bleak and lonely outpost—passenger and goods figures for here would make very interesting reading. I wonder did children travel here by train to attend the Thurlstone School Board's Hazlehead school, which today is home to the Hazlehead Activity Centre? Pictured here are the old station buildings of Hazlehead, still standing the test of time nearly 50 years after closure.

Wednesday, 27th December, 1995

The station at Hazlehead has lived a chequered life to say the least. It was first opened on May 1st, 1846, by the S.A. & M. but when the M.S. & L. Ry took over in January, 1847, the company became increasingly short of money and one of their many cut backs was to close Hazlehead Station—on November 1st, 1847.

Three years later, in November, 1850, the station re-opened complete with a new name, Hazlehead Bridge. After exactly 100 years of serving a scattered community the station closed in March, 1950.

Sunday 26th April, 1998

Leaving Dunford Bridge the 19-mile journey to Sheffield is along a falling gradient of between 1 in 135, and 1 in 100. This tastefully restored stone overbridge can be seen when travelling alongside Thurlstone Moor on the approach to Hazlehead.

Sunday, 9th June, 1996

Pictured here are the overgrown trackbed remains of a lost moorland railway which once linked the main Woodhead line with the Hepworth Iron Company's works. This company came into being late in the 1850s, the line was constructed a few years later, in 1861, to carry coal, fire clay and iron ore.

The Hepworth Branch was only a short 1½ mile single line, but it was steeply graded (1 in 23). Its most interesting feature was a tunnel approximately ¼ mile in length that burrowed beneath the moorland shale. The line closed in 1960 and today little remains, apart from this shallow cutting, an embankment, and a bridge over the nearby River Don.

Sunday, 26th April, 1998

In December 1997, Barnsley council, with the aid of a government grant, paid contractors to demolish Hazlehead Bridge. Their reasoning was that it was a nuisance and an inconvenience for the heavy goods vehicles, and there was the added risk of 'bridge bashing'!

As these two pictures illustrate, when the 150-year-old bridge was demolished, visibility for motorists was greatly improved, so much so that many drivers were tempted to travel at high speed. The official limit on Whams Road is 60mph, but 80mph plus is common!

On Sunday, August 16th, 1998, a 26-metre steel bridge was lowered into position as part of improvements to the Trans-Pennine Trail. The new bridge, which gives more clearance over the road, will be used by horse riders and pedestrians.

Sunday, 15th November, 1998

Before leaving Hazlehead, one more view of the area from a nearby field. In this picture the new Trans-Pennine Trail bridge over the A616 is now in position, but also of interest is the embankment of the old Hepworth branch clearly illustrating the severity of the climb.

BULLHOUSE

Wednesday, 27th December, 1995

Continuing along the Upper Don Trail, passing alongside the long-abandoned Bullhouse Colliery site as wintry, late afternoon sunshine catches the old trackbed in sombre mood.

Over the years, mine-water pollution has been seeping into a four-mile stretch of the nearby River Don, colouring the river bottom orange and smothering all life. But, with the help of a £1 million experimental project using natural methods to filter iron oxide, it is hoped any remaining impurities will be removed from the river, thus helping fish and other wildlife to recolonise this stretch.

Sunday, 26th April, 1998

The third of four obstacles to negotiate on the journey between Manchester and Sheffield, this one due to the demolition of the bridge at Bullhouse, on Sunday, March 20th, 1988.

If you had been standing in this same spot on the afternoon of July 16th, 1884, you would have been looking at a scene of total carnage. The 1230 express from Manchester, hauled by 4-4-0 No. 434 was derailed here after a crank axle on the loco gave way. The coaches following went down the embankment and were smashed, tangled and twisted. Tragically 24 people were killed and 33 seriously injured. Rescuers tended to the dying and injured on Thurlstone Road and Bullhouse Lane. The scene was depicted in the *Illustrated London News*.

SHORE HALL
LEVEL CROSSING

Wednesday, 27th December, 1995

Two miles from Penistone is Shore Hall Level Crossing and it is interesting to note that at this point sections of trackwork survive, the first *in situ* since Hadfield. The rails have been left as part of the modern 'Polymer' type level crossing.

In Woodhead's final years, millions of pounds were spent on modern track and maintenance—what a waste!

THURLSTONE
LEVEL CROSSING

Tuesday, 20th January, 1998

Late wintry sun highlights the old railway crossing at Thurlstone, again with rails *in situ*. This is the point where Hornthwaite Hill Road crosses over the track-bed, it is a similar view to that which the signalman would have had from Thurlstone Signal Box.

PENISTONE GOODS

Wednesday, 27th December, 1995

Entering Penistone past the old Goods Yard. This was the site of Penistone's first station, which opened for traffic on Monday July 14th, 1845. Note the original stone coal drops, six in total, complete with Buffer Stops.

PENISTONE STATION

Sunday, 22nd February, 1998

The present Penistone Station was opened by the M.S. & L. on February lst, 1874, at a cost of £9,200. An agreement was reached with the L. & Y. Ry for them to pay £200 annually as their share of working expenses at the new station which, incidentally, was constructed with seven platforms. With the opening of this station, Penistone's first station became goods only.

I am pleased to say that most of the station buildings at Penistone survive and are used by various small companies including a wholesale wine merchant, a pine and antique business and a computer firm. The large white building (top left) is now the property of Lavender, a metal testing company, but from 1954–81 it was home of the Penistone Electric Control Station, which controlled all Manchester–Sheffield–Wath electrified railway lines.(See map on page 14.)

Wednesday, 18th February, 1998

Today, only two of the original platforms survive in use. Here, departing from platform 2 (formerly No. 5) is the 0728 Sheffield–Huddersfield service, whilst awaiting departure on the up-platform—No. 1 (formerly No. 6) is the 0739 Huddersfield–Sheffield service.

Tuesday 6th January, 1998

Early in 1993, work was started on the refurbishment of Penistone Station's platforms and buildings. Included in the work was the provision of two heated waiting shelters, surrounding landscape work and restoration of the original M.S. & L. canopy which covers part of platform 2.

An official ceremony was held after the refurbishment work was completed. Councillor J. Meredith, re-opening the station on Thursday, July 29th, 1993. Pictured here is part of the surviving M.S. & L. cast lettering which has been restored and is believed to be in the original livery.

Friday, 20th March, 1998

Directly after leaving Penistone Station, Huddersfield-bound trains cross the high and impressive 29-arch Penistone viaduct. Pictured rumbling across this curved structure is the 0838 departure from Sheffield. Also visible in this picture is Emley Moor television mast which, at 1,084ft is the tallest free-standing structure in the UK.

PENISTONE

Sunday, 5th April, 1998

In the year 2000, on July 1st, the railway between Penistone and Huddersfield will celebrate its 150th anniversary. This 13$\frac{1}{2}$ mile route was originally authorised as part of the Huddersfield & Sheffield Junction Railway in June, 1845, and through the line's construction it amalgamated with the Manchester & Leeds Railway, becoming part of the Lancashire & Yorkshire Railway in 1847.

Departing from Penistone and leaving former L. & Y. rails behind, is the 1715 Huddersfield–Sheffield service, a three-car Class 144 in West Yorkshire Metro livery.

Wednesday, 18th February, 1998

The 0706 Huddersfield–Sheffield service heads into the misty morning sunrise shortly after its departure from a cold and frosty Penistone Station.

Also in this picture, taken only weeks before its closure, is Penistone Signal Box (Huddersfield Junction). Under the Railtrack re-signalling programme for the Barnsley area, (Easter weekend, April 9th–14th, 1998) Penistone signal box was closed after the end of services on Thursday, April 9th, 1998.

Monday, 2nd June, 1997

The signal box was re-named in 1989, and also in that year (June and July, to be exact) all the remaining electrification stanchions between Penistone and Barnsley Junction were removed, leaving Huddersfield Junction in splendid isolation.

Sunday, 22nd February, 1998

Huddersfield Junction Signal Box dates from 1886 and is an M.S. & L. Ry Type 2 (variant design) originally boasting 64 levers. In its final years, however, it operated on a meagre 8 levers!

One of the last people to operate the box was G.C.R.S. member Karl Pashley—and his faithful Lakeland Terrier, Basil.

CHURCHYARD OF ST JOHN THE BAPTIST

IN MEMORY OF

CHARLES FRETWELL THE SON OF
JOHN AND ELIZABETH FRETWELL
OF PENISTONE GREEN

WHO LOST HIS LIFE WHILE ON DUTY AT
OXSPRING STATION
ON THE 14th DAY OF JUNE 1853
AGED 27 YEARS

WATCH THEREFORE FOR YE KNOW NOT WHAT HOUR
YOU LORD DOTH COME, MATTHEW, XXIV, CH 42V

IN AFFECTIONATE REMEMBRANCE OF

BE YE ALSO READY FOR IN SUCH AN HOUR AS YE THINK NOT THE SON OF MAN COMETH

FOR THINE IS THE KINGDOM

JONATHAN KAY SON OF GEORGE & MARY KAY OF
DUNFORD BRIDGE WHO DIED FEBRUARY 19, 1877
AGED 26 YEARS
ALSO OF EMMANUEL KAY SON OF THE ABOVE
GEORGE AND MARY KAY WHO DIED MAY 11th 1877
AGED 20 YEARS
ALSO OF MARY WIFE OF GEORGE KAY
& MOTHER OF THE ABOVE WHO DIED
FEB 11th 1890 AGED 60 YEARS
ALSO IN EVER LOVING MEMORY OF
THE ABOVENAMED GEORGE KAY
OF DUNFORD BRIDGE WHO DIED MAY 25th
1910 AGED 86 YEARS
HE WAS FOR MANY YEARS STATION MASTER
AND SERVED THE GREAT CENTRAL RAILWAY Co
FAITHFULLY FOR 55 YEARS AT DUNFORD STATION
AND WAS HIGHLY RESPECTED BY ALL WHO KNEW
HIM.

INTERRED AT PENISTONE CEMETERY
MAY 28th 1910

LIFE'S WORK WELL DONE
LIFE'S JOURNEY WELL RUN
LIFE'S CROWN WELL WON
NOW COMES REST.

Whilst researching local history in St John the Baptist's church I came across two interesting railway-related gravestones. Many of the early gravestones refer to Penistone as 'Peniston' and spelling mistakes seem quite common—whether this was due to lack of space on the headstone, or simply a stone mason's error I do not know.

Sunday 22nd February, 1998

Land once occupied by the Cammell Laird steel works which was founded on this site in 1863 and, at its peak, employed 1,500 men.

When Cammell Laird expanded, a new works was constructed on the opposite side of the Great Central Railway with both sites linked by a standard gauge tunnel. In 1930 the complex closed, but it was later developed as a foundry by the David Brown company who made high-pressure steam turbines for the power industry. In later years that company, too, closed and the area became derelict. I am glad to say that the tunnel has recently become visible again, due to clearance work in preparation for a new housing estate.

PENISTONE, BARNSLEY JUNCTION

Sunday, 1st March, 1998

Thankfully, at least some industries survive in the Penistone area and wherever I am, when the opportunity arises, I try to incorporate these sites in my photographs to give more of an overall view of the area.

Approaching the former site of Barnsley Junction, the 1315 Huddersfield–Sheffield service gathers speed along the former Great Central main line.

Wednesday, 9th August, 1998

Unfortunately, the journey on the second part of the surviving Great Central between Manchester and Sheffield is over all too quickly—covering a distance of only some 962 yards to be exact!

The section of line between Barnsley Junction and Deepcar was closed on May 16th, 1983, and, from that date, all passenger services between Sheffield, Penistone and Huddersfield were routed via Barnsley. Heading for that town is the 1127 Huddersfield–Lincoln Central service.

OXSPRING

Sunday, 1st November, 1998

Continuing the journey now on foot past the old Willey Bridge Junction, under Back Lane and Roughbirchworth Lane, to the site of Oxspring Station.

Oxspring Station opened in December, 1845 but, like the first Hazlehead station, was closed two years later due to M.S. & L. cutbacks. Sadly, the station never re-opened for passenger use but continued for goods only.

RUMTICKLE

Sunday, 7th March, 1999

Having passed Blackmoor Crossing, it is a short distance to the impressive Rumtickle Viaduct which crosses over the River Don.

Across Rumtickle Viaduct is the secluded and picturesque hamlet of Rumtickle. With a little imagination, even though it was only open two years, 1845–47, it is easy to picture the forgotten Thurgoland Station in the deep cutting here.

This photograph (taken in pouring rain) clearly shows the restoration work of Romtickle House (note the different spelling) which I believe was once the local inn, built in 1845, presumably to serve Thurgoland Station.

RUMTICKLE VIADUCT

Wednesday, 18th February, 1998

Recently I heard of an incident that occurred during construction of the viaduct, further research proved the story to be true as this picture shows.

A stone block was built into the structure containing the inscription:

WM. CRAWSHAW
KILLED BY THIS STONE
JULY 6th, 1844

William Crawshaw was a navvy employed in construction of the Sheffield, Ashton-under-Lyne and Manchester Railway. Tragically, this particular stone fell on him and claimed the poor fellow's life. Subsequently, his workmates carved this suitable inscription.

It took me over two hours of slipping and sliding up and down the steep embankments to locate the stone—I still bear the scars to prove it. All the time I was searching, Thunder sat patiently looking up at me as if to say 'Just look at him—what's the silly bugger up to now?' It was worth it in the end though.

The river bank here makes an ideal spot for a rest, flask of tea—and the inevitable digestive biscuits!

THURGOLAND TUNNEL

Sunday, 26th April, 1998

Thurgoland Tunnel, or as it was originally called, Huthwaite Tunnel.

The tunnel is ¼ mile long and was, in engineering terms, called a 'drunken' referring to something not constructed accurately. So, following the lay of the tunnel opening, to obtain maximum clearance, the rail levels of both tracks actually had to differ!

In 1944 the L.N.E.R. decided to open out Thurgoland Tunnel in preparation for electrification but, due to geological problems, a second 350yd tunnel was constructed alongside the original.

Ten years later, in September, 1954, Electric Traction eventually reached Sheffield Victoria.

Today, the original Thurgoland Tunnel is blocked, leaving the L.N.E.R. tunnel for walkers and cyclists alike to pass through—remember your torch!

THURGOLAND BRANCH

Wednesday, 19th August 1998

Having safely negotiated the tunnel, the Woodhead route once again opens out into glorious countryside.

I must mention here the M.S. & L. 2-mile Thurgoland Colliery Branch that once ran to Stainborough. This line which opened in November, 1847, was originally intended to extend to Chapeltown. The line branched middle right of this picture.

WORTLEY CUTTING

Wednesday, 12th June, 1996

A deep ½ mile cutting on the approach to Wortley Station. This section of trackbed has been impassable in winter months due to flooding since the closure of the line between Penistone (Barnsley Junction) and Deepcar 16 years ago.

You can see from this summer photograph what a tremendous vantage point this place must have been for watching the trains.

WORTLEY

Sunday, 20th December, 1998

In total contrast to the previous picture, a winter view of the same cutting and half a mile of impassable trackbed! Looking at this it is hard to imagine that this was Britain's first all-electric main line!

WORTLEY STATION

Sunday, 8th October, 1995

Closed to passengers in May, 1955, and nearly half a century on it still survives—or at least the up-platform buildings do!

These Wortley Station buildings date from 1888. A date stone and M.S. & L. Ry coat of arms still survive, just like we saw at Newton.

STOCKSBRIDGE BYPASS

Sunday, 8th October, 1995

In 1988, the A616 Stocksbridge Bypass opened, a fast dual carriageway which links the M1 Motorway with the A628 Woodhead Pass.

A new road, so what is so special about that? But, just look what this £18 million road blocks—the Woodhead Route. What, with the Woodhead Tunnel blocked, most of Crowden's Permanent Way unrecognisable, the loss of bridges at Hazlehead and Bullhouse, this is the last straw—and the last of five major obstacles to be overcome before Woodhead could ever possibly re-open!

DEEPCAR

Sunday, 8th October, 1995

4¹/₂ miles after leaving the old Barnsley Junction, the iron road can be joined again for the remaining 8-mile run to Sheffield. Before that, however, it is worth a detour down the Stocksbridge Railway, a 1¹/₂ mile branch line which was opened in April, 1877, to serve Samuel Fox's steel works.

Sunday, 7th September, 1997

The two main engineering features on the Stocksbridge Railway are the bridges which span the River Don and the Deepcar to Wortley road.

In 1989, these two bridges were strengthened to allow heavier scrap waggons and B.R. loco's to work into the complex. At the same time the exchange sidings were closed down.

Class 56029, passes the redundant sidings and is about to cross high above the River Don.

STOCKSBRIDGE

Sunday, 13th July, 1997

Class 56091, brings a Sunday afternoon working from Aldwarke New Site into Ellencliffe Loop, today's exchange point between E.W.S. loco's and the steelworks' engines.

The waggons that will be exchanged are loaded with cast carbon-steel 'blooms' from the Aldwarke site at Rotherham. These steel blooms will then be taken into Stocksbridge Works for rolling into 'rounds' before being returned to Aldwarke by rail.

Sunday, 7th September, 1997

Class 56029 crossing the impressive strengthened bridge over the River Don, with the 6J52 to Aldwarke New Site, with its rake of heavy steel rounds.

Between Stocksbridge (Ellencliffe loop) and Sheffield, train services operate using a single-line token obtained from Woodburn Junction signal box. 30mph is the maximum speed permitted between Deepcar and Woodburn Junction.

Monday, 16th May, 1988

With green-carded waggons out of the way and examiners satisfied, the rake of waggons is properly checked and prepared.

Class 20045 (leading) and 20135 are about to depart with the evening 'tripper' back to Tinsley.

Sunday, 8th October, 1995

This picture, taken seven years later, shows the drastic demise of Deepcar, with the sidings ripped up, signal box vandalised and the station buildings in a state of near collapse—a sad sight indeed.

I am pleased to report that the station has been tastefully restored, complete with working station clock. Deepcar Station closed to passengers on June 15th, 1959.

WHARNCLIFFE

Sunday, 25th January, 1998

From Deepcar and on through the delightful Wharncliffe Woods but, before reaching Oughtibridge, I must mention the Ewden Valley Works Railway.

After years of negotiations, designs and acts, in 1913 the Sheffield Corporation began a project to construct two reservoirs in the Ewden Valley, one at More Hall and a higher one at Broomhead.

On leaving the Great Central Railway, on the down side, just north of Wharncliffe Wood signal box, the line entered exchange sidings and, following a reversal, the single line climbed with severe gradients for over two miles up this secluded valley.

The first notable engineering feature after leaving Wharncliffe Exchange Sidings, is this girder bridge of three spans over the River Don. The 1914-18 war delayed construction of the reservoirs, but eventually both opened in 1929. The branch was severed from the main line in 1935 and subsequently the whole line was dismantled. Looking at this view I can easily imagine a Manning Wardle locomotive trundling over!

Sunday 29th October, 1995

One final picture of the Deepcar area, and Thunder. This is on the picturesque Wharncliffe Crags which overlook Deepcar Station.

OUGHTIBRIDGE

Sunday, 28th May, 1995

Oughtibridge Station opened in July, 1845, with the larger station building a later addition, and was closed to passengers in June, 1959. Like so many other small stations years ago, Oughtibridge boasted an active goods business including coal merchants, pulp traffic for the local mill, scrap metal, and busy timber traffic from nearby Wharncliffe Wood.

That busy railway activity is just a distant memory now. Recently, even South Yorkshire Tarmacadam Limited vacated their station building offices which had been their home since May, 1983.

Oughtibridge Signal Box closed on May 14th, 1983, it was the last gas-lit signal box in the Sheffield Division.

Sunday, 15th June, 1997

In appalling weather conditions Class 56088 passes through the station, with the 1855 Deepcar–Aldwarke New Site.

About five minutes before I took this picture, I passed two youths out rabbiting with dogs, I informed them that a heavy freight train was due but, with a couldn't care-less attitude, they walked on down the track regardless of the danger. I heard the driver of this speeding train sound his horn and I guess the trespassers scattered just like their hunted rabbits!

BEELEY WOOD

Sunday, 22nd June, 1997

Exactly one week later, on the same Deepcar–Aldwarke diagram, I caught 56088 on film again, passing through the picturesque Beeley Wood. After waiting to capture this picture for well over three hours in pouring rain, I was eventually rewarded at precisely 1838.

After walking back with Thunder, down through Beeley Wood and over the River Don, for the bus to Sheffield, we found that the rain had been so heavy that Middlewood Road North was badly flooded—even the ice cream van was jingling 'Rain Drops Keep Falling On My Head'!

Sunday, 28th May, 1995

At Beeley Wood Level Crossing are a few surviving Sheffield, Ashton-under-Lyne & Manchester stone sleepers. 150 years ago they would have been fastened to sections of 16ft wrought iron rails, supported with keyed 'chairs'.

WADSLEY BRIDGE

Sunday 28th May, 1995

Goods traffic at Wadsley Bridge ceased in May, 1983, and in early 1986 the railway sidings were removed all except for the 'down' goods loop. This was retained as a run-round for football specials and today is operated by a ground frame.

Sunday, 18th May, 1997

Load Haul liveried class 56084 approaching Wadsley Bridge with the 6G58 Deepcar–Aldwarke service. The retained down goods loop is clearly evident in this picture but sadly it is rarely used. Saturday January 8th, 1994, was the last time a football special used this facility.

Saturday, 15th June, 1996

Wadsley Bridge Station appeared and disappeared from the public timetable, on the same dates as Oughtibridge.

The signal box at Wadsley Bridge was located on the up-platform, it closed in 1985. The key for operating both ground frames is kept safely at Woodburn Junction Signal Box. After closure, the box and derelict station buildings became a hideout for vandals and glue sniffers, then, following a few years of decay and neglect, British Rail finally demolished the once-splendid buildings in March–April 1988, at a cost of £25,000!

Earlier, I mentioned the up-platform and buildings being swept away early in 1988. That's not exactly true because a short section over Halifax Road survives to this day. Wadsley Bridge Signal Box was located just to the left of this picture.

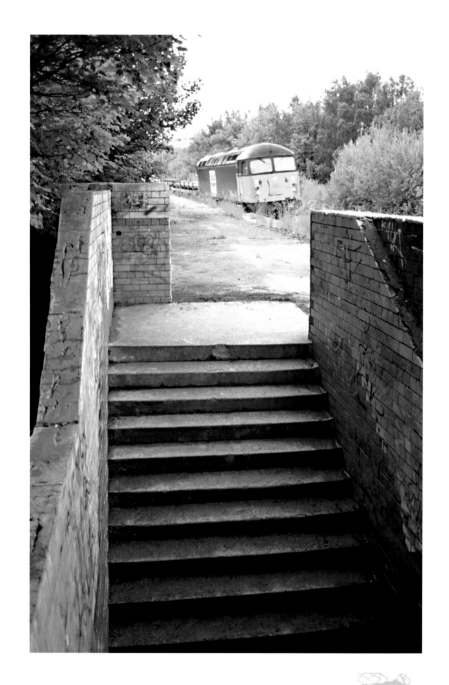

Sunday, 29th June, 1997

The station's subway is now blocked off, but it still retains an attractive tiled stairway which led football supporters from the lone down platform to Sheffield Wednesday's Hillsborough Stadium.

Class 56084 with the Deepcar–Aldwarke working passes through disturbing the peace.

WARDSEND

Thursday, 14th April, 1988

Returning from Deepcar with an engineer's special to Beighton Permanent Way depot, Class 97413 is seen passing through Wardsend cemetery on the approach to Neepsend.

I read a letter, from Colin Fetch, in the Sheffield *Star* that said Wardsend must be the only cemetery in England which has a railway running through it. I think I must agree!

NEEPSEND

Thursday, 14th April, 1988

Taken from the same position as the previous picture, but facing the opposite direction. Here a pair of Class 20s returning to Tinsley from Deepcar, passes the site of the former Neepsend Power Station.

Saturday, 15th June, 1996

Photographed from the now lost railway community of Parkwood Springs looking down towards the site of Neepsend Station, both a late-comer and early casualty on the railway map.

There were plans for a station here from as long ago as 1857, and several attempts to proceed but, due to bickering between Sheffield Corporation and the Manchester, Sheffield & Lincolnshire Railway, Neepsend Station didn't open until July 1st, 1888. In railway terms the station was short lived, closing 52 years later on October 28th, 1940.

Sunday 28th May, 1995

There are plenty of railway related structures still surviving around the Neepsend area, amongst the most impressive are the former coal drops. In its day, in contrast to this quiet Sunday morning, the once surrounding cobbled streets must have been alive with the hustle and bustle of various Sheffield coal merchants.

Saturday, 15th June, 1996

From high above Neepsend, close to the Sheffield Ski Village, looking down on an area once dominated by the railway industry, including the Neepsend locomotive shed.

Darnall Depot replaced the cramped Neepsend Engine Shed in 1943, during World War II.

RUTLAND ROAD, SHEFFIELD

Monday, 31st March, 1997

Rutland Road is crossed just under a mile from journey's end at Sheffield Victoria. From street level, on the corner of Boyland Street, the remains of Sheffield No. 1 Signal Box can be seen.

PITSMOOR ROAD, SHEFFIELD

Saturday, 15th April, 1989

1999 marked the 10th anniversary of the Hillsborough disaster, a tragic loss of life at a football match. Saturday, April 15th, 1989, started off a beautiful spring day with glorious sunshine. That day I was out and about early photographing around the Sheffield area, and my plans had been to capture the only football special conveying Liverpool supporters to the lone platform at Wadsley Bridge Station.

Obviously the special train hauled by Class 47 No. 47434 which was named *Pride In Huddersfield* is pictured travelling in the opposite direction to our journey, but inclusion of the special is my tribute to all 96 people who lost their lives on that fateful day.

Prior to 1909 in this view, with the impressive backdrop of brickwork, would have been Pye Bank Tunnel.

SPITAL HILL TUNNEL

Friday, 14th June, 1996

Before crossing the Wicker Arches, a short 301yd diversion down through the steeply graded 1 in 36 Spital Hill Tunnel. This single line bore was inspired by the Sheffield & Rotherham Railway and finally built by the Midland Railway, opening in January, 1847.

The tunnel's purpose was for the exchange of freight traffic between the Midland's Wicker goods and the M.S. & L. yard at Bridgehouses. The tunnel was closed completely in 1949, several suggestions were made for its future use but none materialised.

Sunday, 7th February, 1999

A very interesting find for me, whilst partaking in a recent walk organised by the Yorkshire Branch of the Railway Ramblers, was this original Midland Railway boundary post standing high and proud overlooking the Bridgehouses end of Spital Hill Tunnel. I'm glad to say, this 152-year-old railway artefact nestles in the rock amongst tufts of grass—hopefully well away from any vandal!

Sunday 7th February, 1999

Another view of Spital Hill Tunnel, this time photographed from the surviving cobbled entrance on Brunswick Road. In October, 1978, Sheffield's Royal Hospital closed and was subsequently demolished. It is reputed that rubble from the demolition was deposited inside the old tunnel!

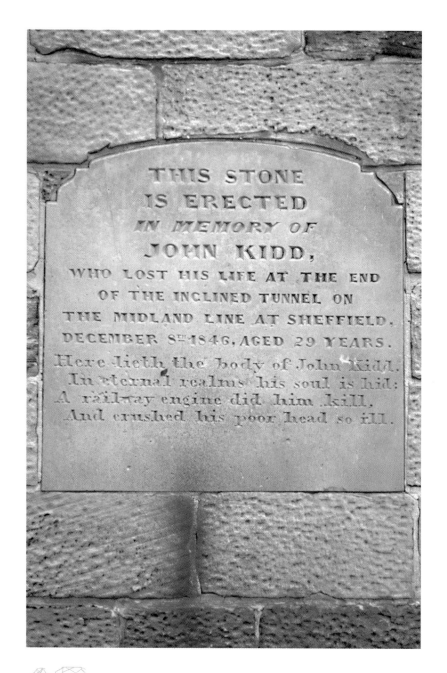

MEMORIAL TO JOHN KIDD

Sunday, 10th August, 1997

This stone was erected in memory of John Kidd, who lost his life at the end of the inclined tunnel on the Midland line at Sheffield, December 8th, 1846, aged 29 years.

Here lieth the body of John Kidd
In eternal realms his soul is hid
A railway engine did him kill
And crushed his poor head so ill

Today, John Kidd's gravestone, amongst others, can be seen outside Morrison's supermarket, adjacent to the main Langsett Road, Hillsborough.

Friday, 24th July, 1998

Standing on the corner of Spital Hill and Carlisle Street, I obtained this picture by pointing my camera over the high retaining wall which today protects a large garage complex and many car showrooms. The east end of Spital Hill Tunnel is bricked-up but is still clearly visible.

This area of land was once the site of Sheffield's first railway station—the Sheffield & Rotherham Railway's Wicker Terminus, which was opened in October, 1838. The Wicker station closed to passengers in February, 1870, and afterwards became goods only, it remained in use for nearly 100 years, until complete closure in July, 1965.

WICKER ARCHES

Wednesday, 12th July, 1996

In order to capture this view I set my alarm for 3 a.m. and walked via the Sheffield & Tinsley Canal to arrive at the Wicker Arches just as the first rays of sun were about to highlight this masterpiece of Victorian civil engineering.

A coat of arms is located above each of the two pedestrian tunnels, on the left is the M.S. & L. Ry insignia, and on the right that of the Earl of Yarborough graces the structure.

Also of note, inside the left pedestrian tunnel, is the memorial to the employees of the Great Central Railway who lost their lives in the First World War. On this bronze plaque 1,304 names are listed (see pages 151–155). To me it seems a sad place to locate a war memorial.

In December, 1940, when Sheffield was being blitzed by the *Luftwaffe*, a bomb actually made a direct hit on the main Wicker Arch. Fortunately, the bomb never exploded after crashing through the stonework, though the scars are still visible to this day.

Wednesday, 1st January, 1997

Wicker Arches, this time photographed on New Year's Day. The freshly fallen snow adding atmosphere to what is, without doubt, Sheffield's finest railway structure.

The two coats of arms on this side of the 72ft arch, again located above the pedestrian tunnels are, on the left, those of the Duke of Norfolk and, on the right, the Sheffield coat of arms.

Surrounded by a complex of road networks, resembling a spiders web of tarmac, this, my last photograph, says it all—a locomotive with no traffic, surrounded by railway neglect. But for how long? The Government must act soon to pump the necessary millions of pounds into our forgotten and overgrown weed-riddled trackbeds. Most importantly, any plans must include— *Woodhead–The Lost Railway.*

SHEFFIELD VICTORIA

Sunday, 21st September, 1997

Class 56059, working the 6G60 Deepcar–Aldwarke New Site crosses the Wicker Arches and is about to pass through the former site of Sheffield Victoria Station.

Monday, 31st March, 1997

The Royal Victoria Hotel, which opened in September, 1862, adjoining the station, was operated by the Sheffield Hotel Company. From 1890, it became railway owned. Then nearly 100 years later, this and other railway hotels were all sold off to private concerns.

Today, the 'Royal Vic' is run by Holiday Inns and is currently undergoing a £1 million refurbishment programme. Importantly, the restoration work on the hotel will retain its majestic Victorian appearance.

WOODHEAD - THE LOST RAILWAY

Stephen Gay

Forty miles of railway splendour
from Manchester to Sheffield on a journey to remember,
leaving the city of bustle behind
we pass through Gorton, Godley and Hyde.

Over the viaducts of Mottram and Dinting,
just as our train catches the sun's rays glinting,
onwards past Hadfield we speed along
towards an area of beauty and song.

Ahead are shining silvery rails
as we pass beside the splendour of vales,
along the Pennine Way and keeping to time
with gradients stiff and hard to climb.

With the Woodhead Tunnel in our sight
we remember the navvies who built with their might,
tons of gunpowder to blast their way
through an engineering feature of the day.

Over three miles of darkness under Woodhead terrain
goes coal, steel and the passenger train,
emerging from Woodhead into daylight we pound
along the iron road that's maintained safe and sound.

Descending through Dunford we quicken the pace
our coaches follow suit swaying with grace,
about the remote station of Hazlehead we chatter
then over points and crossings through Penistone we clatter.

A wave from a Ganger as we continue our quest
passing a long heavy freight slogging up west,
speeding through stations with beauty and wonder
our train cuts off from its mighty thunder.

Then enters an area heavy in pride
built around industry with Victorian stride.

The end of our journey is near complete
as we cross the Wicker arch of seventy-two feet,
a Sheffield landmark built with elegance and class,
but I'm afraid it's all a dream now via the Woodhead Pass!

MEMORIAL TO
GREAT CENTRAL RAILWAYMEN

The bronze plaque, in memory of Great Central Railway employees who gave their lives for their country 1914-18, is in a dark pedestrian tunnel beneath Sheffield's Wicker Arches. The plaque should never have been placed here, it looks uncared for, dirty and goes unnoticed by most people—apart that is from the attentions of vandals and senseless yobs!

On August 9th, 1922, Field Marshal Earl Haig unveiled the plaque in its prominent position outside Sheffield Victoria station. Then, prior to Armistice Day in 1939, it was relocated to the station booking hall. Sadly, Victoria Station closed on January 5th, 1970, and the memorial was relocated again to its present site, with a rededication service held on November 10th, 1971.

I hope that in the near future this historical bronze plaque will once again be displayed in a more prominent and fitting location, one more respectful of those 1,304 G.C. railway workers who made the supreme sacrifice.
Lest we forget!

IN MEMORY OF GREAT CENTRAL RAILWAYMEN
WHO GAVE THEIR LIVES IN THE GREAT WAR 1914–1918

ABBEY • C
ACKERS • A
AINSWORTH • F
ALDRIDGE • W • J
ALLCOCK • R
ALLCOCK • W • H
ALLEN • F • R
ALLEN • W
ALLEN • W
ALLEN • W • O
ALMOND • A
ALMOND • W
ALSOP • F
AMES • A
ANDERSON • J • W
ANDREW • A
ANDREW • H
ANDREWS • C • F
ANDREWS • J • A
ANGEL • H • J
ANYON • G
ARDON • J • A
ARIS • W • E
ARKWRIGHT • A
ARKWRIGHT • T
ARRAND • B
ASH • F • A
ASH • V • E
ASHCROFT • F
ASHTON • J • E
ASHTON • S
ASHTON • T
ASPLEN • A
ASTON • D • G
ATACK • P
ATCHISON • J • S

ATHERTON • W
ATKIN • G
ATKINSON • H • T
ATKINSON • P • G
ATKINSON • W
ATTWOOD • E
ATTWOOD • W • H
AUSTIN • J • (MM&BAR)
BACKHOUSE • A • L
BACKHOUSE • W • H
BACON • A • E
BAGNALL • H
BAGWELL • H
BAILEY • J
BAILEY-WESTOBY • H
BALDWIN • C
BALL • F
BAMFORD • J
BAMFORD • T
BANCROFT • J
BANNISTER • J
BANNISTER • S • P
BANYARD • E
BARBER • C
BARBER • R
BARKER • F
BARKER • G
BARKER • J • W
BARKER • W
BARLOW • H
BARLOW • R • A
BARNARD • W
BARNARD • W • H
BARNES • F
BARNES • J • L
BARRETT • F • C

BARRETT • J
BARTLE • P • F
BARTRAM • V • G
BASELEY • F
BATE • W
BATHE • P • J
BAXENDALE • H
BEACOCK F • J
BEAN • A
BEAN • F
BEARDSMORE • C • J
BEELEY • J
BEEVER • G • H
BEEVERS • S
BELL • A • E
BELL • R • S
BELL • W • H
BELLAMY • C
BENNETT • C • L
BENNETT • H
BENNETT • H • Y
BENNETT • J
BENSON • J
BENT • A
BENTLEY • E • S
BENTLEY • T
BERRY • A • H
BERRY • J • F
BERRY • W
BEST • T
BEST • W • F
BESTWICK • A
BEVERLEY • E
BEVITT • G
BEXON • H
BICKNELL • E

BIMSON • J
BINGHAM • J • F
BIRD • W
BIRKINSHAW • C
BIRTLES • S
BISHOP • L
BISHOP • W
BISPHAM • W
BISWELL • S • G
BLAKELEY • J
BLANCHARD • J • A
BLANDEN • L
BLANEY • A
BLIGH • J • W
BLOW • G • H
BLUNDELL • L • E
BLYTHMAN • A
BOARDMAN • R
BODEN • G • (MM)
BODSWORTH • G • W
BODYCOTE • T
BOHANNA • E
BONNER • G • E
BONNET • R
BOOT • J • A
BOOTH • J • E
BORMAN • F
BORMAN • S
BORRILL • J
BOSTOCK • S
BOTTERILL • A
BOTTOM • W • B
BOULTON • C • H
BOWDEN • A • E • P
BOWDEN • F • J
BOWDEN • J

BOWDEN • S • J
BOWLER • L
BOWNESS • S • M • (MM)
BOWTELL • C • R
BOYD • R
BOYLE • T • J
BRACKENBURY • W • J
BRACKLEY • H • G • H
BRADBURN • H
BRADBURN • W
BRADBURY • W
BRADLEY • A
BRADLEY • F
BRADLEY • H • S
BRADSHAW • W • N
BRAID • J • W
BRAMMALL • E • W
BRAMMER • A
BRAND • A
BRANNAN • A • G
BRASSINGTON • J
BREARLEY • A • E
BRIDGER • G • A
BRIDGES • L • A • F
BRIGGS • J
BRITTAIN • J • W • S
BROADBENT • H • W
BROCKLEHURST • E
BRODERICK • A
BROOKBANK • W • A
BROOKES • W
BROOKES • J
BROUGH • J
BROWN • A
BROWN • F
BROWN • H

BROWN • W • H
BRUMBY • J • H
BRUMUND • E
BRYSON • W • R
BUCK • A • L
BULL • A
BULLAS • J
BURBRIDGE • W
BURFIELD • W • A
BURGAN • T • A
BURGESS • A
BURGESS • G • M
BURGESS • W
BURGESS • W
BURKE • D
BURKET • C
BURNEY • J • H
BURREL • H • E
BURROWS • F
BURROWS • W
BURTON • A
BURTON • J
BURTON • J • T
BUSWELL • P
BUTLER • J
BUTLER • N
BUTLER • W • M
BUTTERFIELD • J
BUXTON • B
BYFIELD • W
BYROM • J
CAIN • M
CALCUTT • C • R
CAMM • H
CAMMACK • W • S
CARPENTER • W • E
CARRATT • E • R
CARROLL • R
CARRUTHERS • K • L
CARTER • A
CARTER • A • S
CARTER • F
CARVER • C
CASE • J • T
CASEMORE • W • J

CATHERALL • E • (DCM)
CATLEY • R • W
CATTERALL • J
CAUDWELL • C • J
CAUSER • J
CHADDERTON • E
CHAFER • H • J
CHAMBERLAIN • E
CHAMBERS • W
CHANEY • W • H
CHANT • T • H
CHAPMAN • F • W
CHAPMAN • J • A
CHAPMAN • W
CHARLTON • R
CHATTERTON • A • F
CHAUNDY • J • H
CHEESEBOROUGH • H
CHEETHAM • S
CLAPSON • H • B
CLARK • C • J
CLARK • W
CLARKE • F • G
CLARKE • L • W
CLARKE • S • W
CLARKE • W
CLAXTON • E
CLAYTON • H
CLAYTON • L • W
CLEAVER • R
CLEMENTS • R • B
CLOUGH • J
CLUTTERHAM • A • A
COCKCROFT • W
COCKELL • E
COLBRIDGE • A
COLES • H
COLES • J • W
COLLEY • J • (MM&BAR)
COLLIER • A • G
COLVILLE • H • E • L
COMRIE • G • M
CONEY • H
CONNAH • L
CONNOLLEY • M

CONNER • F
CONROY • W • E • G
CONSTANTINE • J
COOK • C • C
COOK • F
COOKE • A • H
COOKE • C • G
COOKE • E • N
COOPER • A
COOPER • J
COOPER • W
COOTE • R
COPE • W
COPPEN • S
COPPOCK • S
CORRIGAN • J
COSMAN • E
COULTAS • R • M
COUPLAND • W
COURTNEY • W • C
COUSINS • W
COVELL • E
COWLING • J • W
COX • F
COX • G
COX • G • B
COX • L
COZENS • F
CRACKLE • W
CRAFT • T
CRAMP • C
CRANCH • G
CRANFIELD • W
CRATE • I • R • E • (MM)
CREASE • J
CRICK • R
CROFT • G • W
CROFTS • H
CROOK • E • W
CROSSLAND • S
CROSSLEY • A
CROSSLEY • C • V • (DSC)
CROWCROFT • A
CRUTTENDEN • W • N
CUMBLIDGE • J • H

CUMMINGS • H
CUNNINGHAM • P
CUTHBERT • A
CUTLER • J • R
CUTTS • W
DAKIN • G
DALE • S
DALES • A
DALES • W
DANIELS • C
DAVIES • A
DAVIES • E
DAVIES • G
DAVIES • J
DAVIES • J
DAVIES • J • J
DAVISON • S • (DCM)
DAWKES • A • E
DAWNEY • C
DAWSON • J • W
DAY • F
DAY • J • E
DAY • R • B
DEAN • A
DEARNLEY • G • H
DEARY • T
DEMELLWEEK • J • J
DENNERLEY • L
DENNISON • C
DEPLEDGE • F
DERNIE • W
DEVAN • J • H
DEWSON • W • G
DEXTER • S
DIBB • E • V
DICKENSON • J • W
DICKENSON • R
DICKENSON • G • H
DICKENSON • H
DICKENSON • J • L
DILLON • J
DISNEY • J
DIXON • F • (DCM)
DIXON • F
DIXON • W

DODD • C • V
DOOLEY • J • P
DORAN • J
DORAN • T
DORBER • E
DOUGHTY • W • W
DOVE • W
DOWAN • J
DOWNEND • A • V
DOWNS • A
DRINKHALL • E • E
DRIVER • L
DUFFILL • G
DUFFY • C • J
DUFFY • H
DUFFY • T
DUNDERDALE • T
DUROSS • H
DURR • J
EADY • W • T
EAST • H
EDDLESTON • H
EDMONDS • G
EDWARDS • A • J
EDWARDS • A • L
EDWARDS • F • W
ELLIOTT • B
ELLIOTT • E • C • J
ELLIOTT • H • C
ELLISS • W • H
ELSOM • J • T
ELTON • R • H
ENDERBY • A
ENGLAND • J
ENTWISTLE • W
ERNILL • W
ERRATT • C
EVANS • G • H
EVANS • H • E
EVANS • I • (MM)
EVANS • T • J
EYRE • H
FANSHAWE • F • C
FANTHAM • H
FANTHORPE • B

FANTHORPE • F • C
FANTOZZI • A
FARR • G
FARRAND • F
FARRELL • R • J
FARROW • H
FAWCETT • J • R
FEATHERSTONE • E
FELL • F
FENTON • G
FERN • W
FEWKES • C
FIELD • J
FINNINGLEY • A
FISHER • R
FITZPATRICK • D
FITZPATRICK • J • J
FLETCHER • T
FLINT • J
FLOWER • C • S • (DCM)
FLYNN • J
FORSTER • F
FOSTER • F
FOULKES • J
FOWLER • B
FOX • R
FRANCIS • E • T
FRANKLIN • A • J
FRANKLIN • L • R
FRITH • J
FRYER • C
FULLER • T • A
GADSBY • H
GALLEY • R • G • E
GARBUTT • J • D
GARLICK • F
GARRATT • J • F • W
GARRETT • W • A
GARSIDE • H
GARWELL • E
GIBB • G • C
GIBBONS • G • F
GIBBS • G • E
GIBSON • J
GIBSON • W

GILES • G • E
GILL • A • W
GLASSEY • T • J
GLOVER • T
GODBOLD • H • G
GODDING • A • V
GODFREY • E
GODSALL • G • T
GOLDING • R
GOODEY • E
GOODFELLOW • A
GOODMAN • C • W
GOODMAN • J • V
GOODMAN • W • H
GOODWIN • J • H
GOSTELOW • C
GRAEBURN • G • W
GRAHAM • C
GRANT • A
GRANT • F • W
GRANT • L • J
GRASSBY • W
GRAVILL • A
GRAYHURST • A
GRAYSON • W
GREARLEY • T
GREAVES • F
GREAVES • F • W
GREEN • C • M
GREEN • J • C
GREEN • S • E
GREENFIELD • J • H
GRAY • A • S
GRIFFITHS • W • A
GRIFFITHS • W • J
GRIMSHAW • A
GRIMSHAW • S • E
GUEST • B
HAGUE • E
HAGUE • J
HAGUE • T
HAKIN • H
HALEY • J
HALL • H
HALL • T

HALL • T • E
HALLAM • T
HALLIWELL • E
HALLS • F • P • W
HAM • H • P
HAMER • R
HAMILTON • A • E
HAMLET • S
HAMLET • T
HAMLETT • C
HAMMOND • H • C
HAMMOND • L
HAMMOND • S
HAMPSHIRE • H
HAMPSON • J
HAMPSON • J
HANCOX • J • W
HANSON • H
HARDING • W • T
HARE • H • V
HARGRAVE • H • N
HARRINGTON • E
HARRINGTON • W
HARRIS • C • J
HARRISON • E
HARRISON • R
HARRISON • W • J
HARROP • H
HART • E
HART • W
HARTLEY • H
HARTWELL • F
HARVEY • A
HARWOOD • J
HAUGHTON • A
HAWES • R
HAWKINS • F
HAWKRIDGE • E
HAY • H • J
HAYES • A
HAYES • W
HAYNES • F
HAYWARD • J • H
HEAD • E
HEADLAND • H • E

HEALEY • J • B
HEAPS • G • W
HEATH • G
HEATON • J
HECKLER • A
HEDGES • W
HEENEY • A
HEGINBOTTOM • J
HELLIWELL • N • J • W
HEMPSTOCK • J
HENSHAW • G
HEPPLESTONE • J • W
HERCOCK • S
HETHERINGTON • A • W
HEWITT • G • E
HEWITT • W
HEYES • T
HEYWOOD • A
HIBBITT • A
HIGGINBOTTOM • F
HIGGINBOTTOM • G
HIGGINS • E
HIGGINS • J • P
HILL • J • W
HILL • W • N
HILLSON • J
HILTON • A
HILTON • P
HILTON • R
HINCHSLIFF • W • H
HINTON • J
HITCHCOCK • J
HOBBS • R
HODDER • H • A
HODGE • J
HODGETTS • H
HODGKINSON • J
HODGKISON • C • M
HODGSON • G
HODGSON • S
HODSON • F
HODSON • H
HOGG • F
HOLDEN • A
HOLLAND • F

HOLLINGSWORTH • A
HOLMES • C
HOLMES • J • P
HONOUR • A • J
HOOD • E
HOOKER • W • A
HOPE • S • R
HOPKINS • F
HOPKINS • J • H
HORNBUCKLE • L • C
HORNBY • W
HORNSBY • E • S
HORSFALL • J
HORSLER • W • A
HOUGHTON • G • W
HOUSHAM • G • W
HOWARD • F
HOWARD • G • A
HOWARD • J
HOWARD • P
HOWARD • W
HOWARTH • C
HOWELL • W
HOWES • W • L
HOWSON • A
HUCKER • N
HUDSON • A
HUGGARD • A
HUGHES • E
HUGHES • W • G
HULME • C • V • T
HUMPHREYS • J
HUNSTONE • W • H
HUNT • G
HUNT • G • A
HUNT • W
HUNT • W
HUNT • W • H
HUNTER • H
HURLEY • V • P
HURST • H • H
HUTTON • C
HUTTON • T • H
IBBOTSON • C
IVES • J

JACKLIN • W
JACKSON • E • A
JACKSON • F
JACKSON • H
JACKSON • J • T
JACKSON • S
JACKSON • S
JACKSON • W
JACKSON • W
JACKSON • W
JANNEY • A • B
JARVIS • H • F
JAYES • J • W
JEAVONS • A
JEFFERY • H
JEFFREYS • J
JEFFERIES • C
JEFFS • W • A • H
JENKINS • C • W
JENKINSON • F
JENNINGS • J • E
JENNINGS • T
JESSOP • G • H
JOHNSON • A
JOHNSON • A
JOHNSON • F • L
JOHNSON • H
JOHNSON • H • D
JOHNSON • T
JOLCLIFFE • J
JOLLEY • A
JONES • B
JONES • E
JONES • E
JONES • G
JONES • T • H
JONES • W
JUBB • S • F
KEELING • J • W
KEELTY • T
KELLER • A • G
KELLY • R
KELLY • S
KEMP • H • R
KENDALL • J • A

KENT • E
KENYON • H
KERSHAW • H
KEYWORTH • J
KILLERBY • J • F
KING • J • H
KIRBY • J
KIRK • W
KIRMAN • C
KIRMAN • T
KITCHEN • T
KITCHING • G
KNIGHT • E
KNOWLES • W
LABBETT • J
LAKE • F • H
LAMB • H
LAMB • H
LAMBERT • F • W
LAMBLEY • W
LAND • G • W
LANG • G
LANGHAM • B
LARSON • C
LAWLEY,T
LAWTON • C
LAZENBY • F • (MM)
LEE • A
LEE • D
LEE • G • W
LESTER • H
LEVI • C • T
LEWIS • A • E
LEWIS • H
LINDLEY • J
LINGARD • S
LITCHFIELD • H
LIVINGSTON • F • M
LIVINGSTONE • A
LLOYD • T
LOBLEY • W
LOCKE • H
LOCKING • J
LOOKWOOD • H
LOMAS • F

LOMAS • J
LONG • G • W
LONGSON • J
LOVE • J
LOVETT • W • A • F
LOVETT • W • T
LOWE • A
LOWE • A • R
LUCAS • P
LYON • B
MACARTHUR • E • F
MACDONALD • J
MACHIN • J
MACKERETH • E
MACKINTOSH • C
MAINWARING • E
MAINWARING • W
MALKINSON • H
MALPAS • E
MALTBY • H
MANSHIP • A • H •
MARKHAM • G
MARKHAM • G • C
MARNEY • E
MARPER • R
MARRIS • H • F • (MC)
MARSHALL • C
MARSHALL • R • F
MARSLAND • C • F
MARSLAND • G • R
MARTIN • W • F
MARWOOD • C • H
MASDIN • H
MASHETER • T
MASON • J • W
MASSEY • L
MASSEY • W
MATHER • W • H
MATHEWS • J • F • C
MATTHEWMAN • B
MATTHEWMAN • W
MATTHEWS • F
MATTHEWS • J • V
MARUICE • S
MAW • F

MAWHOOD • A • E
MAYCOCK • G
McCABE • J
McCARTHY • A • D •
McCRACKEN • C
McCULLOCH • A
McGINN • E • T
McKELVEY • H
McKENZIE • W
McKIERNON • S
McLAUGHLIN • J
McLAY • A
McMURRAY • W
McPHUN • H
McPHUN • R
MERCER • E
MERRYWEATHER • J
MESSOM • A • G • F
MICHAEL • A • B
MICKLETHWAITE • H
MIDDLETON • O
MIDGLEY • W • R
MILLER • G
MILLER • P
MILLNS • J
MILNES • B
MITCHELL • C
MITCHELL • G • A
MICHELL • R
MONKS • M
MOORCROFT • E
MOORE • G • W
MOORE • H
MOORE • H • M
MOORE • J
MOORE • J • E
MOORE • T
MOOREWOOD • E • H
MOREMAN • G
MORLEY • F
MORRIS • F
MORRIS • F
MORRIS • H
MORRIS • H • C
MORRIS • J

MORRIS • J • S
MORRISON • J
MORTON • H • R
MOSS • E
MOULD • J • S
MUGGLESTONE • C
MUMBY • T
MURRELL • G • C
MYCOCK • A
NADEN • A • W
NADEN • W
NALL • W • D
NAYLOR • J • H • R
NAYLOR • T • (MM)
NEGUS • F
NEILD • D
NELIGAN • D • W
NELSON • G
NETTLETON • W
NEWEY • H
NEWMAN • H
NEWMARSH • H
NEWTH • R
NEWTON • F
NEWTON • N • G
NEWTON • W • J
NICHOLSON • A
NICHOLSON • G
NICHOLSON • J
NICHOLSON • J • T
NORBURY • R
NORRIS • J • M
NORRIS • R
NORTON • F
NORTON • S • G
OAKDEN • J • A
OAKES • G
OAKES • M
OGDEN • H
OGG • C • A
OGILVIE • A
O'GORMAN • F
OLBY • R
OLDHAM • J • H
OLIVER • H • W

ORRELL • J • T	PLATT • T • B	RICHARDSON • S • S	SCOFFINS • T	SLATTERY • J • T
O'SHAUGHNESSY • P	PLATT • W	RIDER • F	SCOTT • A	SLEAFORD • F
OVERTON • W	PLIMMER • J	RITCHIE • J • B	SCOTT • A	SMART • H • R
OWEN • H • R	PLOWRIGHT • L	ROBERTS • E	SCOTT • L • W	SMITH • A
OWENS • W	POCOCK • E	ROBERTS • H • H	SCOTT • S • L	SMITH • A
OXLEY • J	POGSON • J	ROBINS • J • W	SCOTT • T	SMITH • E
OXLEY • P	PORTER • H • C	ROBINSON • C	SEABORN • B	SMITH • E
PACEY-HUTCHINSON • S • H	PORTESS • G • H	ROBINSON • C • E	SEMLEY • C • E	SMITH • G • H
PALEY • M	POULSTON • W	ROBINSON • C • H	SENIOR • A	SMITH • G • W
PALMER • M	POWELL • G • A	ROBINSON • E	SENIOR • C	SMITH • H
PALMER • T	PRICE • J	ROBINSON • G • W • C	SENIOR • J • W	SMITH • H • C
PARKER • A	PRICE • O	ROBINSON • J	SENIOR • M	SMITH • I
PARKER • E • E	PRIKE • J	ROBINSON • W • H	SEWELL • J	SMITH • J
PARKER • H	PRIOR • W	ROGERS • J • W	SHARP • F • J	SMITH • J • W
PARKER • W	PROCTOR • S	ROLFE • D • H	SHARPE • H • L	SMITH • N • H
PARKIN • G	PUDNEY • C • (MM)	ROSE • C • E	SHARPLES • N	SMITH • R • L
PARKINSON • T • A • C	PURKESS • A • J	ROTHWELL • H	SHAW • A	SMITH • S
PARKES • A	PURKESS • C • L	ROURKE • T	SHAW • G	SMITH • S
PARMENTER • W • H	PURKIS • C	ROWARTH • E	SHAW • W • H	SMITH • S • G
PARSONS • F	RABBITT • H	ROWBOTTOM • J • A	SHEEHAN • J • J	SMITH • T
PARTINGTON • H	RANCE • W	ROWELL • F • C	SHELDON • G • C	SMITH • W
PARTRIDGE • H	RANDALL • F	ROWLAND • H • F	SHENTON • G	SMITH • W • G • (MM)
PATTINSON • G	RANSHAW • W	ROWLEY • F • H	SHEPHERD • E	SNELL • E
PAYNE • A • E	RANYARD • R	ROYLE • E	SHEPHERD • F	SNELL • T
PEACH • J • W	RANYARD • W • W	RUSH • J • W	SHEPHERD • J • H	SOLSBURY • W • H
PEARSON • A	RAPSON • J • W	RUSS • F • G • (MM)	SHEPPARD • G • W	SOUTHERN • G
PEARSON • H	RATCLIFFE • R • S	RUSSELL • E	SHERWOOD • J • C	SOUTHERN • H
PEARSON • M • T	RAWLINSON • H	RUSSELL • G	SHIRBON • W	SPEAKMAN • T
PEATE • J • P • B	RAWLINSON • J • E • (DCM)	RUSSELL • H	SIDEBOTTOM • J • W • (MM)	SPEED • T
PENDLETON • S • H	RAYTON • J • J	RUSSELL • J • T	SILLS • G • H	SPENCER • A
PENFORD • R	REDFERN • W	RUTLAND • C	SIMONS • A	SPENCER • G • (MM)
PERCIVAL • A	REDHALL • A	RYDER • E	SIMPSON • G • A	SPENCER • H • L
PERCIVAL • G • F	REED • A	SALISBURY • T	SIMPSON • S • W	SPITTLES • A
PERROTT • W • H	REEDER • G	SALMON • W • E	SIMS • C	SPOTWOOD • H
PETERSON • R	REGAN • W	SALTER • H • F	SINGLETON • A	STACEY • A • V
PETTS • T	RENNEY • A • C • H	SAMPSON • R	SISSONS • G • W	STACEY • L
PHILBURN • J	RENSHAW • J • W	SAUNDERS • A • E	SKEATH • W • R	STAINES • J
PHILLIMORE • W • H	REVILL • P	SAUNDERS • R	SKELTON • J	STAINSBY • G
PHILLIPSON • M	REYNOLDS • E	SAVAGE • A	SKELTON • W • J	STAMP • T
PHILLIPSON • P	REYNOLDS • F	SAVILLE • F • J • R	SKITTY • J • E	STAPLEY • W • H
PHYTHIAN • W • E	RHOADES • G	SCALE • C • A	SLACK • S	STARKEY • J
PICKERING • B	RHOADES • J	SCATTERGOOD • T • V	SLADE • G	STATHAM • L • F
PICKERING • G	RICHARDSON • F	SCHOFIELD • H • B	SLATER • E	STAVELEY • S
PICKFORD • A	RICHARDSON • F • A	SCHOFIELD • S • G	SLATER • G • H	STEAD • F
PICKLES • F • A • (MC)	RICHARDSON • L • H	SCOFFIELD • J • H	SLATER • J	STEAD • H

156

STEAD • T
STEEL • J • A • (MM)
STEELE • J
STENTON • E
STENTON • O
STEPHENS • H
STEPHENSON • C • H
STEWART • J
STILLWELL • T • B
STILTON • G
STOCKDALE • A • E
STOCKTON • T
STOCKWELL • A • E
STOTHARD • E • R
STOTT • W • A
STRATTON • A • E
STRICKLAND • J
STUBBS • C • H
STUBBS • V
STURGEON • C • R
SULLIVAN • G
SUMMERS • A • H
SUMMERS • J • W
SUTTON • A
SUTTON • H
SUTTON • J • T
SUTTON • W
SWANN • J
SWANSBURY • F • (MM)
SWIFT • C • E
SYMONDS • E • H • (MM)
TALBOT • C
TALLIS • G • F
TALLON • T
TASKER • F
TATTERSALL • J • B
TAYLOR • D
TAYLOR • F
TAYLOR • G • F
TAYLOR • J
TAYLOR • J
TAYLOR • J
TAYLOR • R
TAYLOR • W
TAYLOR • W

TEAT • H
THOMAS • E
THOMAS • G
THOMPSON • J
THOMPSON • J
THOMPSON • S • W
THOMPSON • W
THORNDYKE • H
THORNSBY • H • S
THORPE • A
THORPE • P
TIFFANY • S
TILSTON • J
TINSLEY • R • P
TINSLEY • S
TIPPER • W
TOFT • J
TOFT • J • H
TOLSON • H
TOMKINSON • W • J
TOMLINSON • H
TOMLINSON • J • W
TOMLINSON • W
TOOLE • J
TOON • J • A
TOOTILL • W
TOTTEN • W • H
TOWLEY • H
TOYNE • A • W
TRIVETT • C • R
TROOP • J • W
TRUST • E • H
TUCKER • S
TUGWOOD • J
TUPLING • A
TURLEY • R
TURNER • G • M
TURNER • J
TURNER • J • W
TURNER • T • A
TWEED • A
TYERMAN • W
UPTON • V • B
VAUSE • T
VEARY • A • J • H

VERNON • F
VESSEY • J • W
VICKERS • G • H
WADDINGHAM • A • (MM)
WADDINGTON • T • F
WADE • G • H
WADE • S
WAGSTAFFE • F
WALDUCK • L
WALKDEN • W • C
WALKER • C
WALKER • C • W
WALKER • F
WALKER • G
WALKER • H
WALKER • H
WALKER • J
WALKER • J • H
WALKER • P
WALKER • S
WALKER • V • A
WALKER • W
WALLER • A
WALLHEAD • F
WALLIS • C • H
WALLIS • H • C • (MM)
WALSHAW • H
WALTON • A
WALTON • G • T
WALTON • L
WARBURTON • K
WARBURTON • S
WARD • G • A
WARD • G • A • E
WARD • S
WARDELL • F • J
WARDEN • R • E
WARDLE • A
WARHURST • W
WARNEFORD • P
WARNER • J
WARNES • R • H
WARREN • E
WATERFIELD • G • A
WATERHOUSE • T

WATERS • A • F
WATKIN • H
WATKIN • T
WATKINSON • T
WATSON • F
WATSON • S
WATSON • W • R • S
WATTS • H
WATTS • S
WAYNE • R
WEAVER • T
WEBSTER • A
WEBSTER • B • J
WEBSTER • W • B
WESLEY • M
WESLEY • W • H
WESSELDINE • W
WEST • A • E
WEST • A • E
WESTALL • A
WESTON • H
WEYMAN • H • M
WHEELER • A • C
WHEELER • H • (MM)
WHETTON • H
WHINNIE • P
WHITBY • A • W
WHITE • G
WHITE • H
WHITE • J
WHITE • R
WHITE • T • A
WHITEHEAD • H
WHITEHEAD • L
WHITTING • W • H
WICKSON • G • H
WIDDOWSON • E
WILD • J
WILD • J • P
WILDGOOSE • R • C
WILKINS • J • R
WILKINSON • J • F
WILKS • J
WILLERTON • C
WILLIAMS • C

WILLIAMS • F
WILLIAMS • G
WILLIAMS • I
WILLIAMS • J
WILLIAMS • W • H • F
WILLS • J • E
WILLMAN • D
WILSON • B
WILSON • C
WILSON • G
WILSON • G
WILSON • W
WINN • F
WINTER • C • H
WISEMAN • C • R
WITHAM • F • S
WITTY • W • S
WOOD • A
WOOD • C
WOOD • H
WOOD • J
WOOD • J • H
WOOD • M
WOOD • W
WOOD • W
WOODFORD • G
WOODS • E • J
WOODS • H • E
WOODWARD • S • W
WOOLFE • G
WORLAND • A
WORRALL • S
WORTHINGTON • G
WRAGG • W
WRIGHT • G
WRIGHT • H
WRIGHT • J • W
WRIGHT • W
WRIGHT • W • H
WRINGE • A
YORK • W • T
YOULE • E
YOUNG • P
YOUNG • T • G

Stephen Gay with Thunder
(Courtesy of Sheffield Newspapers.)

THE GREAT CENTRAL RAILWAY SOCIETY

Stephen Gay is currently Northern Area Representative of the Great Central Railway Society, a society which promotes the study of this Railway, its constituents and its history under the L.N.E.R. and B.R. The G.C.R.S. was formed in 1974 and has a membership widely spread throughout this country and abroad. Besides those with a general interest in the railway, members include railwaymen, authors, railway modellers and others who are specialists in particular aspects of the G.C.R.

The flagship of the society is the illustrated and professionally produced quarterly journal, *Forward*, which contains regular articles on locomotives, traffic, stations, loco sheds, signalling, personalities, modelling and current news etc. The society operates an extensive archive containing maps, plans, timetables, photographs and other historical documents. Prints and copies of most of the archive items are available to members.

On the social side, the G.C.R.S. has area groups which hold regular meetings, and national seminars are held around the country. All meetings feature talks and or slide shows, usually of unpublished material, together with a range of archive photographic material for perusal and sale.

Finally, other than greatly admiring their achievements and having quite a few members in common, the G.C.R.S. has no connection with the Loughborough-based Great Central Railway.

If you are interested in the society, why not write for further information and a sample issue of *Forward*?

THE GREAT CENTRAL RAILWAY SOCIETY
c/o THE MEMBERSHIP SECRETARY
41, SPIRE HOLLIN
GLOSSOP
DERBYSHIRE
SK13 9BJ